God's
ULTIMATE INTENT

And God said,
Let us make man in our image,
after our likeness:
and let them have dominion . . . .

A Textbook to teach and guide the conception, growth, and development of the Spiritual Formation of a child of sovereign God; and to understand and participate in being in the Image of God and being transformed into the Likeness of Jesus Christ.

By
Francis W. Grubbs, Ph.D.

Library of Congress Control Number: 2017949974
ISBN-13:   Paperback: 978-1-64045-803-1
            PDF: 978-1-64045-804-8
            ePub: 978-1-64045-805-5
            Kindle: 978-1-64045-806-2

Printed in the United States of America

**LitFire**
PUBLISHING

LitFire LLC
1-800-511-9787
www.litfirepublishing.com
order@litfirepublishing.com

TABLE OF CONTENTS

Prologue

We are about to enter a holy chamber of earth's history where Creator-God has for five days been speaking above the empty void of darkness, and chaos of formless matter. He spoke to darkness and called for light to create days and nights and time. He called for a firmament, which He named heavens; gathered the waters under the heavens to form seas—land appeared which He christened Earth. He commanded the Earth to bring forth grass, herbs, trees— all yielding seed. He set the sun to light the day, and the moon to shine at night; then added stars also. He called to the oceans to bring forth sea creatures—from whales to snails, to populate their great depths; and winged fowl to fill the airy heavens. In thunderous voice He commanded them to multiple and fill ocean depths and airy heights.

As day six dawn appeared, He turned to the Earth with one last command: "Bring forth cattle, beasts, and creeping-crawling things—all able to reproduce after their kinds!" He paused, bent down, grasped a handful of earth in His right hand and raised it just above His heart. His left hand touched his brow and He seemed to ponder for a moment. He raised his face upward toward the rising sun—and shouted with a thunderous voice reverberating throughout the universe "LET US MAKE MAN IN OUR IMAGE AFTER OUR LIKENESS, AND LET HIM HAVE DOMINION OVER THE FISH OF THE SEA, AND OVER THE FOWL OF THE AIR, AND OVER THE CATTLE, AND OVER ALL THE EARTH, AND OVER EVERY CREEPING THING THAT CREEEPETH UPON THE EARTH."

He then went down upon His knees, placed the handful of earth upon the ground and with His fingers formed and fashioned a doll-like form replicating His very visage. He then bent low until lips of omnipotence touched lips of clay—He breathed and man became a living soul. A created life-form in the *image* of Creator-God.

Perhaps, my emotions ran a little past the Biblical descriptions of the first six days of earth's history, but the revealed truth is clear: God's vision, plan, and purpose for man was in the mind of God preceding man's creation. This plan, hinged upon the two descriptive words IMAGE and LIKENESS, forms the dimensions of man's being and doing. Man would be in the genus and character of sovereign God. A third word, "dominion" shapes his vocation and role in the eternal kingdom of God.

This Textbook, <u>God's</u> <u>Ultimate</u> <u>Intent</u>, is designed to teach individual members of this family of man, truth, that unlocks the entire Biblical revelation. God did not say let us create man in our *image* after our *likeness*, He said *"Let us make man . . ."* God's creation of man failed due to man's inabilities and the limitations of creations. God, however, foreknew the shortcomings of both man and creations; and He had a continuing plan to make man in His image—He would conjugate with the family of Adam and make a man, not by creation, but by spiritual procreation.

The major thesis of this Textbook begins when an individual human, by faith, embraces Jesus Christ as his or her personal savior from sin, and the holy Spirit of God conceives a spirit being within the inner recesses of that person. This inner man now needs to be nourished, trained, taught, and developed. The Bible provides spiritual food for nourishment, and concepts, precepts, and principles to be mastered by the developing mind. Spiritual formation is a term we use to provide Biblical instruction for every phase of growth and development of the growing child of sovereign God housed in a womb of soul and body. The summary goal of each human being is to be made into the *image* and *likeness* of sovereign God.

These are the themes to be developed, studied, and applied throughout this book, but there is one more facet of teaching and learning that must be acknowledged. We often speak of teaching, learning, knowing . . . without thoroughly understanding what these fully mean. When we say, "I know . . ." do we mean I perceive, I comprehend, or I understand? The same thing is true in the Greek language of the New Testament. This language has two main words that mean "to know", and about six more that provide various ranges or levels of knowledge. The word *ginosko* has a range of meanings from I begin to know, I am aware of this knowledge to I have a good knowledge of something. There are two other forms of this word *epiginosko* which means an advanced knowledge; and *gnoosesthe*, which means absolute knowledge. The second word, *oida* means a fullness of knowledge. Jesus used this word when he said, "Ye s*hall know* the truth and the truth shall set you free."

I have used this discussion of knowledge to make one point: knowing is a word providing a range of knowledge from an *awareness* of a fact or concept to a deep *understanding*. Both *epiginosko* and *oida* from the above paragraph may be translated *understanding*. Understanding is an Old English word relating to the degree of knowledge attained by the learner. It is considered by many educators to be the highest form of knowledge. Furthermore, the learner has such a grasp of this knowledge that he can both explain and interpret it as a teacher; he has the wisdom to make proper application; insight to create a perspective noting the value of this knowledge and how it relates to other knowledge—to your own person and reality at large. Relating it to your own person forms an empathetic bond with that knowledge.

With this elevated concept of *understanding* reechoing in your mind, let me encourage you to determine to study, learn, and achieve *understanding* of the objectives of Spiritual Formation. This full knowledge will include an *understanding* of God, what He meant by making man in the *IMAGE* of God, and the Biblical understanding of man in the *LIKENESS* of God.

Lesson One
GOD'S ULTIMATE INTENT

The Bible breaks upon human history with the declaration, *"In the beginning, God . . . ."* In the flash of a giant strobe, time was birthed from the womb of eternity. The word used to convey the concept of *beginning* means first in place, time, order, or rank. It is truly the fountainhead of time—the prime meridian from which to set all clocks. Standing in the doorway to this stage of time is the eternal GOD, introducing Himself as the sovereign *Elohiym*—God above all gods.

The primal act of God in time is stated by the verb *created*. God created the heaven and the earth. God brought into existence the heaven and the earth and all that is contained in them. He is both the first one and the first cause of all existence. All existence must indeed be interpreted and understood in relationship to its Creator. This is what we will later call a Biblical Worldview—all reality understood in its relationship with God.

> A Biblical Worldview is interpreting and understanding all reality by the concept of God.

The first two chapters of Genesis provide a day by day schedule of creation during the first week of time. God cried out for light and light blazed through the darkness revealing a vast ocean of dark foaming waters where the Spirit of sovereign God brooded like winged fowl o'er troubled nest. God spoke again and the heavenly firmament of skies encircled the globe of waters. Next God called for earth's dry land to appear and arise out of the waters which He called seas. To the dry land God commanded grass, and trees, and all vegetation to grow and reseed themselves in repetitive cycles. God then set two great lights in the heavenly firmament to give light by day and by night and to be for signs, seasons, and for days and for years. And then, in probably the greatest understatement of all Scripture is added the fact, *"He made the stars also."*

Into this beautiful orb of blue skies and seas, and green earth God filled the water with sea creatures and the skies with flying fowl, each in its own specie and kind; He called for the earth to be filled with cattle, beasts, and creeping life forms—each in its own specie and kind. Then God reviewed His entire creation, and surely with a smile—pronounced that it was good.

God's Ultimate Intent Introduced

In Genesis one, verse 26 the thinking, planning mind of God is revealed, as the first defining moment of creation, expressing why God had established time and created these heavens and this earth. This *why* breathes purpose and meaning into creation. The Mind of God is revealed—the ultimate desire of God is unveiled as He states His purpose and plan for His crowning creation.

> *Let us make man in our image, after our likeness: and let them have dominion over the fish of the sea, over the fowl of the air, and over the cattle, and over all the earth, and over every creeping thing that creepeth upon the earth.*

Ponder, very carefully, the words God used to describe His ultimate intent. *"Let us make man . . ."* The word *make* is a very broad term which simply means to bring into being without reference to how He would do it. *"Let us make man in our image . . ."* Image means a resemblance, or even stronger, a representative being. Man was to be in the genus of God. Genus means a class, kind, or group marked by common characteristics or by one common characteristic. Since we do not know the total class and form of the being of God,

> Image means in the genus of God. Genus means a class, kind, or group marked by common characteristics.

we cannot totally fathom the ultimate intent of God concerning the form of man. However, we know that God is spirit. But our understanding of spirit is also limited, we usually use spirit to contrast and differentiate from flesh.

Although we do not fully comprehend the form, class, or genera of God we do know that within the mind of God as He declared His ultimate intent for man was the intent to make man in this God-image. As we study this course of Spiritual Formation we believe this image concept will become much clearer. Let us simply accept at this moment the great realization that God's desire for His centerpiece of creation is that man will be in His image—a replica of His class of being.

The second characteristic is described by the word *likeness*. *Likeness* describes moral similitude. It refers to a being demonstrating the character and character traits of God. True likeness to the character of God would

> Likeness describes moral similitude.

demonstrate a life of perfect love, exhilarating joy, tranquil peace, perpetual patience, kindness, goodness, faithfulness, meekness and self control. We could describe such a life as being Godlike.

The third intent of God for man was that he would take care of the earth for God as a steward for God. The word *dominion* means to have absolute authority and control over the earth and its environs. As God delegated this awesome caretaker-task to man, responsibility flowed

> The word *dominion* means to have absolute authority and control over the earth and its environs.

with it. This language of delegation was very specific as he named each category of living things and the earth environment. As He blessed Adam he emphasized man's procreative nature and purpose and He commanded: *"Be fruitful, and multiply, and replenish the earth, and subdue it: and have dominion over the fish of the sea, and over the fowl of the air, and over every living thing that moveth on the earth (1:28)."*

The First Step of Spiritual Formation

In verse 26 God had voiced His ultimate intent for man naming the two characteristics of man, plus man's vocational responsibilities. In verse 27 we have the description of God's follow-through creative activity to begin to make His intent a reality: *"So God created man in his own image, in the image of God created he him; male and female created he them."* The words translated, *"so God created,"* is quite interesting. The Bible only refers to *"image"* in the creative activity of man in Genesis. The word created refers to a formative process of which we see the creation of man in God's image, but no reference of man being in His likeness. Man was in the form and genus of God but his moral similitude was not yet formed.

Being in this image of God certainly implied that he had a will and would need to express choice if his moral character were to be God-like.

The second step in the spiritual formation of man was instituted by God as He placed him in the Garden of Eden (Genesis 2:9-17) and told man to dress and to keep it. Here is man in the image of God beginning his first task of stewardship. Furthermore, the concept of God is expanded as we enter Genesis 2 and the details of man's creation are expanded. The English term "LORD God" combined the terms *Yehovah* with *Elohiym*. *Yehovah* or Jehovah emphasizes the self-existent and eternal nature of God and later we will see this is the name by which Israel will know their God. Thus man's concept of God is being enlarged as God is now seen as a more personal God in His relationship with the man He has created in His own image.

God now commands the man saying, *"Of every tree of the garden thou mayest freely eat: but of the tree of the knowledge of good and evil, thou shalt not eat of it: for in the day that thou eatest thereof thou shalt surely die* (2:17)."

Two special trees stood among the fruit trees in the Garden of Eden: One—the Tree of Life, and the other— the Tree of Death. Only one tree was forbidden with the dire warning—the day thou eatest thou shalt surely die. This is now the very first step in the spiritual formation of the human race to fully achieve God's ultimate intent. He could make them in His image, but He could not make them in His likeness since moral character is an expression of their will, and if will is truly will it must have free expression. The test was, would man will to do God's will as expressed by His command, or would he choose to please his own will and disobey God.

> The test was, would man will to do God's will as expressed by His command, or would he choose to please his own will and disobey God.

It is clear that Adam and Eve did not understand life, and certainly they did not understand death. But a more vital question was, did they understand God. He had revealed Himself as both the Sovereign Creator—God of heaven and earth. He further revealed Himself as the eternal, self-existent God who was their personal Lord. He had provided them everything they needed and had given only one restriction because that tree would give them great harm. Don't eat of the tree of knowledge of good and evil—it will kill you.

Adam and Eve had a clear choice. Eating of the tree of life would have finalized God's creative activity on their behalf since being in the *image of God* they had the potential of being righteous in character in the *likeness of God*. Refusing to be God-like and partaking of the Tree of Death would shatter the God-image—they would surely die.

Progressive Revelation of God

These two opening chapters of Genesis provide not only history of the beginning of time and the days of creation, but they also provide three pictures of God. The Bible, as God's revelation of truth that man cannot discover for himself, is a vast educational treatise. It opens with the development of concepts defining reality. Concepts are mental snapshots providing

> The four components of reality are God, Man (and other created beings), Matter, and time.

verbal pictures of reality. The four basic concepts revealing reality are framed by the responses to four questions: (1) Who, or what is God? (2) Who is man and other created beings? (3) What is matter? And (4) What is time?

The first two chapters responds to each of these questions. The only part of reality not addressed here, but addressed later in the Bible is the question of other created beings such as angels and demons. The reason for this is that Genesis focuses on the origin of earth and man. It references time, it provides definitive responses to the question, What is Man? It is quite clear in its clarification of matter. Let's spend a little thought comprehending how these opening chapters begin to formulate the concept of God.

We have discussed how specific words are used for the names of God which depict a special characteristic of God. *Elohiym,* in the Hebrew text, introduced God as the eternal sovereign God, the first cause and possessor of supreme power and authority. Nothing can be higher than this, and nothing can limit these. The second Bible portrait of God to enlarge our conceptual understanding is found in Genesis 1:2—a scene of chaos, waste and desolation.

Three word phrases portray this chaotic scene: without form, void, and darkness. Two Hebrew words are joined to convey the meaning of *"without form and void"* as *a waste and a void.* One word relates to matter and the other to form. Combining the two denotes a state of utter confusion and desolation, and the third word depicts this confusion and desolation in utter darkness.

The word that introduces this wasteland is the past tense form of the verb "to be." Discussion has raged among Bible scholars since it can be translated "was" as descriptive of the then present state of "being," or it may be translated "became." Some argue that this was simply the first step in the creative action that produced form and order. Others believe this void was the result of a previous creation which had ended in disastrous ruin, such as the result of Lucifer's fall.

We know for certain that in this dark desolate mass of foaming waves, billowing storms, and raging chaos— the Spirit of God is described as a fluttering brooding fowl seeking to bring form and function from this formless mass. The descriptive word expresses the tremulous motion made by the hen while either hatching her eggs or fostering her young. It here probably signifies communicating a vital or prolific principle to the waters. As the idea of incubation or hatching an egg, is implied in the original word, hence, the notion prevailed among some of the ancients, that the world was generated from an egg.

The word *spirit* is the word *for wind* or *breath.* The same concept is applied to the Spirit of God in the New Testament as Jesus described new birth in John 3:8: *"The wind bloweth where it listeth, and thou hearest the sound thereof, but canst not tell whence it cometh, and whether it goeth: so is every one that is born of the Spirit."* The Spirit of God is also described as a mighty rushing wind filling the house and empowering believers on the day of Pentecost.

Notice carefully that the Spirit of God is the powerful agent of both physical creative formation and spiritual formation. Here in Genesis 1:2 He is brooding over physical creation to bring form and function from chaos and confusion. In Genesis 2:7 the creation of Adam is described: *"And the LORD God formed man of the dust of the ground, and breathed into his nostrils the breath of life; and man became a living soul."*

Capture this picture in your mind. Watch carefully, as creator God picked up dust-like particles of earth substance and with His fingers molded and formed the physical body of Adam-man. Watch as sovereign God bends low until lips of omnipotence touch lips of clay and God breathed—it is again the word for spirit—God spirited the breath, or wind, of life—and man became a living soul.

Once again it is the picture of the Spirit of God as the God-agent of creative spiritual formation bringing life and being to lifeless Adam.

The third view of God given in these opening chapters of Genesis is the one we earlier discussed as presented (2:4-22) through the title "LORD God" It is interesting to see the change in the name of God as we come to this portion that presents the details of Adam and Eve's creation, the Garden of Eden and the responsibilities and regulations given to them.

Earlier we suggested that this combination of *Elohiym* and *Jehovah* presented the view of a personal God. Later in our studies we will see Jehovah as the Covenant God of Israel, and to Moses God identifies Himself as the family-God of Abraham, Isaac, and Jacob.

He is now the Creator God in a personal relationship with Adam and Eve. He provided their garden habitat, their daily provision of food, He outlined their responsibilities, and He walked and talked with them in the cool of the day. He was their God in personal relationship.

Note these three portraits of God painted by these three Names: Elohiym, Jehovah, and Spirit. Skeptics have thrived on the name Elohiym since it is a plural noun used with a singular verb suggesting that it hinted of polytheism. However, a repeated theme of the first five books of Moses is that the Lord, thy God, is one God.

Be alert, and watch carefully as the Bible presents the continuing unveiling and progressive enlargement of the concept and person of God as the revelation of these three initial portraits continues.

Spiritual Formation Personalized

It is not only God's desire to have a personal relationship with each individual, it is His ultimate intent that every one of us be transformed into the *image* and *likeness* of Himself.

> Spiritual Formation is the process utilized by the Spirit of God as He draws us to Christ, conceives within us a child of God, and then becomes our teacher, counselor, and enabler to conform us to the likeness—the character of Christ.

Although Spiritual Formation is the work the Spirit of God does within us, we can recognize from the life and experience of Adam that it is dependent upon the will and obedience of man. It is God's intent and will that man be in the image and likeness of Himself, but it can only be achieved if the person being formed and fashioned in this image and likeness be pliable.

Dear student, as you engage in the study of your spiritual formation as presented through the study of God's revealed Word, we already know the ultimate intent of God to transform you into the image and likeness of God—But, what is your intent?

1Now the serpent was more subtil than any beast of the field which the Lord God had made.

And he said unto the woman, Yea, hath God said, Ye shall not eat of every tree of the garden?

2 And the woman said unto the serpent, We may eat of the fruit of the trees of the garden:

3 But of the fruit of the tree which is in the midst of the garden, God hath said, Ye shall not eat of it, neither shall ye touch it, lest ye die.

4 And the serpent said unto the woman, Ye shall not surely die:

5 For God doth know that in the day ye eat thereof, then your eyes shall be opened, and ye shall be as gods, knowing good and evil.

6 And when the woman saw that the tree was good for food, and that it was pleasant to the eyes, and a tree to be desired to make one wise, she took of the fruit thereof, and did eat, and gave also unto her husband with her; and he did eat.

Genesis 3:1-6

Lesson Two
EVIL'S STRATEGIC CONQUEST

We left Adam and Eve in the Garden of Eden which surrounded the Tree of Life and the Tree of the Knowledge of Good and Evil. As Chapter Three opens an intruder enters the Garden in the form of a serpent. Later in the writings of Isaiah (Ch. 14) this personage is identified as Lucifer, Son of the Morning. He is described as one who had been a potentate in the ranks of heavenly personages until pride caused him to rebel. He had declared, "*I will ascend above the heights of the clouds, I will be like the Most high.*" This language of Isaiah is framed to apply to the king of Babylonia but at the same time introducing the former archangel as the great final enemy described by Paul as the man of sin, by John as the Antichrist, and the Little Horn by Daniel.

Ezekiel in describing the Prince of Tyrus (28:13-19) also describes this same personage as having been the anointed cherub that covereth residing in the Eden of God amongst the beauty and riches of precious stones. He is described as having been perfect in his ways until iniquity was found in him. Pride of his beauty lifted his heart, his wisdom was corrupted because of his brightness, and God has cast him down.

This rebel against God now approached Eve in the form of a serpent and questioned her concerning the rules as established by God. "Yea, hath God said, Ye shall not eat of every tree of the garden?"

Eve responded, *"We may eat of the fruit of the trees, but of the fruit of the tree in the midst of the garden, God said, 'Ye shall not eat of it, neither shall ye touch it , lest ye die."*

The rebel serpent responded, contradicting God, "Ye shalt not surely die, God doth know that in the day ye eat thereof, then your eyes shall be opened—ye shall be as gods, knowing good and evil."

Eve, influenced by this subtile snake, saw that the fruit appeared good for food, she heard him say it would make her wise—she tasted the fruit, took some to her husband—they ate in disobedience to God. Immediately they both knew a drastic change in their being. They realized their naked condition and were embarrassed. They heard God coming for their walk together—fear, for the very first time, gripped their hearts.

As God inquired into their condition they both became defensive and denied blame. A dramatic change had come in their lives, as they first experienced the result of sin. God pronounced punishment upon the serpent changing the stately dinosaur-like being into the crawling snake. To Satan he pronounced his final doom, and although he would wound the Seed of the woman, that Seed would crush his head. God placed Eve under the authority of Adam and told her of the pain that would accompany childbirth. Then to Adam God described that the ground would be cursed as a result of man's failure and life would be a constant struggle for survival. Previously, God had warned them, if they ate of the Tree of the Knowledge of Good and Evil, they would surely die. Now God described physical death as *"dust thou art and unto dust shalt thou return."*

God drove Adam and Eve from the Garden and placed a flaming sword and guard of angels to protect Adam and Eve from eating from the Tree of Life and existing forever in this sinful, fallen, degenerative condition.

The Bible portrays this scene as a third person description of what happened. It is as if a newspaper reporter watched what happened and described it. We only see the outward results of what had happened inwardly. The New Testament picks up this same narrative in the first chapter of Romans, but in this text God allows us to view the inward changes resulting from both the sin and His judgment of their disobedience. Here, we will see what Satan had smugly described as their eyes being opened—huge diabolical changes, limitations, and death seized control of minds, bodies, and spirits of the Adamic race and their descendents.

Understanding the Horror of Sin

Although Satan, through the serpent's voice, had made disobedience to God seem like a trite thing with beneficial results, God depicts it as such a destructive and ruinous force causing His wrath to erupt against all ungodliness and unrighteousness of men in flaming fires of judgment.

God begins, through the writings of Paul, to describe the progressively downward disintegration of the mind of man and what happened within the internal personality of man because of his sin.

Because that when they knew God, they glorified him not as God, neither were thankful; but became vain in their imaginations, and their foolish heart was darkened. Professing themselves wise, they became fools and changed the glory of the uncorruptible God into an image made like to corruptible man, and to birds, and four footed beasts and creeping things" (Romans 1:21-23).

Although we have studied that God had revealed Himself to Adam and Eve as the Sovereign Creator, the eternal omnipotent life giving God, who is also a personal provider, they did not honor Him as God. The enticing, lying words of the Tempter made them desire to be like God in knowledge. Rejecting God's intent that they be in His image and likeness, sinful man reimaged God in their image and the downward spiral into foolishness caused them to make gods of animals, reptiles, and insects.

Notice verses 24, 26, and 28 containing three key responses by God to man's rebellious actions.

(24) Wherefore God also gave them up to uncleanness through the lusts of their own hearts, to dishonor their own bodies between themselves: (25) Who changed the truth of God into a lie, and worshipped and served the creature more than the Creator, who is blessed for ever. Amen.

(26) For this cause God gave them up unto vile affections: for even their women did change the natural use into that which is against nature: (27) And likewise also the men, leaving the natural use of the woman, burned in their lust one toward another; men with men working that which is unseemly, and receiving in themselves that recompense of their error which was meet. (28) And even as they did not like to retain God in their knowledge, God gave them over to a reprobate mind, to do those things which are not convenient; (29) Being filled with all unrighteousness, fornication, wickedness, covetousness, maliciousness; full of envy, murder, debate, deceit, malignity; whisperers, (30)

Backbiters, haters of God, despiteful, proud, boasters, inventors of evil things, disobedient to parents, (31) Without understanding, covenantbreakers, without natural affection, implacable, unmerciful: (32) Who knowing the judgment of God, that they which commit such things are worthy of death, not only do the same, but have pleasure in them that do them (Romans 1:24-32).

The language of God's action is *"God gave them up . . . . God gave them up . . . . God gave them over."* Literally God is placing man under a special control system. Man, who had been free to make his own choice concerning whether to obey God and eat of the fruit from the Tree of Life or the Tree of the Knowledge of Good and Evil, now was placed under another system of Control.

I remember as a small lad going out with my dad on the hay rack. We would come to a gate in the barbed wire fence and dad would hand me the reins. I was in control of those mighty prancing stallions (those old plugs), to drive the rack through the gate.

This is the picture of the language of each of these three verses. God turned the reins of control of man over to three control agents. Man was no longer a free moral agent.

Man Controlled by His Psyche

Since man had refused to "glorify God" as God, and had turned to the creature rather than the Creator, God turned the control of man over to what is described in verse 24 as *"uncleanness through the lusts of their own hearts."*

Lusts are demanding *desires* and God is now turning the control of man over to man's own

Psychological Ego Desire System—his psyche. Man would never again face a decision without the clamor of his self- centered psyche demanding to be fulfilled. Isaiah said it well— *"All we like sheep have gone astray; we have turned every one to his own way; and the LORD hath laid on him the iniquity of us all"* (Isaiah 53:6).

The basic motivation of man is "I want my way," and it is true of the 5 year old spitting and stamping and crying, and of the 85 year old demanding, "I'll just leave if I don't get my way."

As God turned man over to this psychological desire system, man entered a prison house of control. His character went from bad to worse as he now substituted the LYE for the TRUTH, turned his adoration to the creature and served it. He turned his veneration and service toward creation away from the Creator. The creature is the world of matter or materials—man became a materialist. This is a theory that physical matter is the only or fundamental reality and that all being, processes and phenomena can be explained as manifestations or results of matter.

Man Controlled by His Physical Body

Secondly, since man, now controlled by his psyche, had changed his view of reality from a God centered to a matter centered reality, God now (vs. 26) turned man over to be controlled by what is described by the English term, *"vile affections"*. The actions described

are sexual sins of men and women, and the introduction of homosexuality. These are physical and fleshly sins.

God has turned man over to the control of his **Biological Drive System**. Man controlled by his Psychological Ego Desire System demanded to have his own way, now controlled by his Biological Drive System he demanded to be satisfied. From this moment on every choice man faced would be motivated by his self-psyche desire system, demanding self-fulfillment; and driven to be satisfied by his drives and appetites.

Man Controlled by Demonic Mind

Man, controlled by his psychological desire system, and his biological drive system had become a humanistic materialists. He now demanded the discard, even of the name and concept of God. Verse 28 describes, *"And even as they did not want to retain God in their knowledge . . . ."*

Man did not want the concept of God in their apperceptive mass. They wanted to expunge Him from their vocabulary, to erase Him from all their books, to blot Him from even the imagery of their minds.

God now turned the final control center of man over to a reprobate mind. A mind totally opposite to God— **A Demonic Mind**. Man, as a spiritual being was now dead—totally separated from God.

Not only is man controlled by psychological ego desires demanding self-fulfillment, his biological drives demanding self-satisfaction, and a demonic mind regulating all learning and all knowledge; but often there is even civil war in his being as one control center tries to out maneuver and overpower another internal control system.

Man created in the *image* of God and designed to be in His *likeness* was now totally opposite that ultimate intent envisioned by God. Man was in a downward spiral going from bad to worse and even worse than that. Struggles raged in his being, sin increased in horror, violence escalated, and his sin and guilt intensified. Out from his life flowed a septic river of sewage described by these verses:

> *(29) Being filled with all unrighteousness, fornication, wickedness, covetousness, maliciousness; full of envy, murder, debate, deceit, malignity; whisperers, (30) Backbiters, haters of God, despiteful, proud, boasters, inventors of evil things, disobedient to parents, (31) Without understanding, covenantbreakers, without natural affection, implacable, unmerciful: (32) Who knowing the judgment of God, that they which commit such things are worthy of death, not only do the same, but have pleasure in them that do them.*

Ponder this last description, not only is a man haunted by his guilt and fear of the death judgment, he still practices the same sins, and more than that, his movies and TV plots feature sex, violence, and murder— they find their entertainment in them that do them.

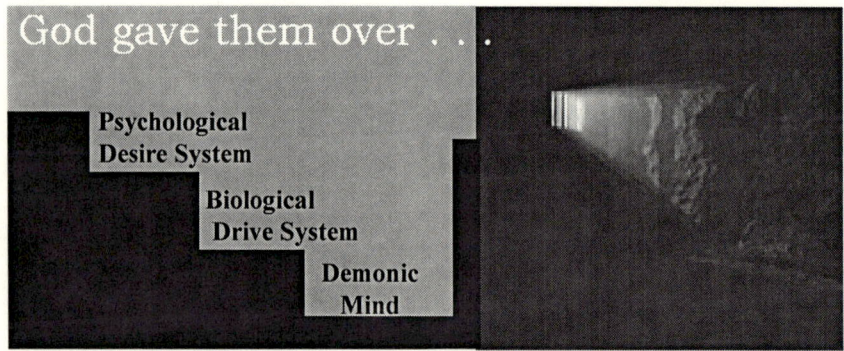

Three Steps Down into the Dungeon of Sin

Fettered Earth and Broken Image

The Book of Genesis opened in a scene of physical chaos with the Spirit of God brooding over it as a troubled fowl over her nest. We watched as God brought order and beauty out of chaos and then declared, *"Let us make man in our image, after our likeness. . . ."*

Enter, the *serpent,* tempting man and the anointed cherub who failed in his quest to be like the Most High and fell from his high position of Star of the Morning, now caused man to fail as a being in the *image* and *likeness* of God. Even a greater question is, did Satan also cause God to fail in His intent to make man in the image and likeness of God?

A second chaos gripped the earth as thorns and thistles ravished the gardens and fields—creation groaned and travailed in pain—the bondage of corruption enshackled the globe.

Chaos invaded the dark recesses of man's soul, controlled by the psychological ego, and disfigured the physical members convulsed by drives and appetites demanding to be satisfied; and raged within the imaginations of the mind and heart spiraling downward in an evil continuum.

Creation, that the sovereign Creator had assessed as "good," groaned in bondage of sin; and man designed in the *image* and *likeness* of God moaned in his miserable dungeon of death—a shattered *image* and a *likeness* devoid of God.

𝔚𝔥𝔢𝔯𝔢𝔣𝔬𝔯𝔢, 𝔞𝔰 𝔟𝔶 𝔬𝔫𝔢 𝔪𝔞𝔫 𝔰𝔦𝔫
𝔢𝔫𝔱𝔢𝔯𝔢𝔡 𝔦𝔫𝔱𝔬 𝔱𝔥𝔢 𝔴𝔬𝔯𝔩𝔡, 𝔞𝔫𝔡 𝔡𝔢𝔞𝔱𝔥 𝔟𝔶 𝔰𝔦𝔫; 𝔞𝔫𝔡 𝔰𝔬
𝔡𝔢𝔞𝔱𝔥 𝔭𝔞𝔰𝔰𝔢𝔡 𝔲𝔭𝔬𝔫 𝔞𝔩𝔩 𝔪𝔢𝔫,
𝔣𝔬𝔯 𝔱𝔥𝔞𝔱 𝔞𝔩𝔩 𝔥𝔞𝔳𝔢 𝔰𝔦𝔫𝔫𝔢𝔡:
Romans 5:12

𝔉𝔬𝔯 𝔞𝔩𝔩 𝔥𝔞𝔳𝔢 𝔰𝔦𝔫𝔫𝔢𝔡,
𝔞𝔫𝔡 𝔠𝔬𝔪𝔢 𝔰𝔥𝔬𝔯𝔱 𝔬𝔣 𝔱𝔥𝔢 𝔤𝔩𝔬𝔯𝔶 𝔬𝔣 𝔊𝔬𝔡;
Romans 3:23

Lesson Three
GOD'S PLAN FOR MAN'S RENEWAL

S tanding astride the rubbled ruin of Adam's failed dominion, the LORD God turned facing the Serpent *"Because thou hast done this, thou art cursed above all cattle, and above every beast of the field; upon thy belly shalt thou go, and dust shalt thou eat all the days of thy life . . . I will put enmity between thee and the woman, and between thy seed and her seed; it shall bruise thy head, and thou shalt bruise his heel"* (Genesis 3:14-15).

God's Curses Upon the Tempter and the Tempted

The language of the Creator's curse upon the serpent was completely opposite to the elevated hope he had described in his temptation of Eve. It was a curse that made the serpent the most vile, detestable creature on earth crawling among the dust dunes of earth. The phrase *"upon thy belly"* is expressive of the lowest stage of degradation to which a spiritual creature can sink. "*Dust shalt thou eat,*" is an indicative of aimless existence.

Eve had already realized the lying deception of the reptile for she said, the serpent beguiled me and I did eat. Now she listened as curses fell from the lips of the LORD God upon that groveling creature. It is interesting to note that while God was directing these curses upon a physical snake its larger import was directed to the fallen cherub as he described the enmity between him and the woman. This serpent is the same that is identified in Revelation 12 as the great dragon . . . that old serpent, called the Devil, and Satan.

A sudden ray of hope blazed from the curse of the Creator as He spoke of the enmity and war between Satan's seed and Eve's seed, *"It shall bruise thy head and thou shalt bruise his heel."* Eve heard that promise and a flicker of hope was conceived within her heart which she would later express at the birth of Seth. *"For God hath appointed me another seed instead of Abel."* Furthermore, her statement, *"God hath appointed him"* recognized this son is from God. She regarded him as God's son. She receives this gift from God, and in faith expected him to be the godly seed to crush the serpent's head.

This ray of hope that brought a little light into Eve's darkness must have reverberated through the Angelic world—God's ultimate intent was not dead. His prophetic words of the woman's seed was the first hint that He was not yet finished with man—the Image and Likeness of God.

God then directed His words to Eve, *"I will greatly multiply thy sorrow . . . ."* She would have pain and sorrow in pregnancy, childbearing, and childraising. She would understand the sorrow of heart for her children's disobedience much like God was now feeling for His disobedient children.

The third part of Eve's judgment was as a wife. She had been created as a partner and help-meet, but since she had taken the lead in transgression, in the fallen state her retribution was placement under the will of her husband. *"Thy desire shall be to thy husband"* is not referencing sexual desire, it literally means, "the determination of thy will shall be yielded to thy husband." The second clause, presented in parallel structure in the sentence serves as a climax or emphatic reiteration of the first: *"he shall rule over thee."* Under the self-serving fallen man controlled by his psychological desire system and his biological drive system, woman has been little more than a slave.

"Adam," God continued, *"because you hearkened unto your wife, and ate of the tree I commanded you not to eat, I curse the ground for your sake."* *(not a direct quote.) Since Adam had been given dominion over the earth, his sin affected the earth and made it, in the words of the New Testament, *"subject to vanity,"* and under the *"bondage of corruption." Vanity* means *frail and dying* and from the fields and meadows thorns and thistles would rule. Adam's life would be a constant challenge for survival until he returned to dust. God had said—*"thou shalt surely die."*

The lie of Satan and the sins of Adam and Eve were now in stark relief as God drove Adam and Eve from their garden home and placed cherubim with flaming swords to guard Eden lest they attempt to return and eat of the *Tree of Life* and live forever in their corruption and sinfulness.

God must have turned to look upon the man and his wife and I wonder if His heart was not breaking for the frail, frightened, naked, children—filled with anguish and remorse. In a striking act of love and concern for those who had failed to fulfill His heart's intent, He killed animals and took their skins to make clothing for the naked couple. I can imagine that tragic scene as the weeping crying man and his wife were driven out into a hostile world with only the skins of dead animals girded about them.

The Formation of God's Plan for Renewal

We must recognize that the fall of man was no surprise to God and that his Plan was formulated in His mind before the foundation of the world. But within the world of time and man it would take centuries for God's plan to renew man and bring about the total fruition of His ultimate intent—man in the *image* and *likeness* of Himself.

The curse upon the serpent was the first hint, not only that God had a plan but that it would come not from creation but from pro-creation. The seed of woman would crush

> The curse upon the serpent was the first hint, not only that God had a plan but that it would come not from creation but from procreation.

the head of Satan. Thirty centuries later this same theme would be filled with greater meaning as Isaiah wrote this great prophetic utterance, *"Therefore the Lord himself shall give you a sign; Behold, a virgin shall conceive, and bear a son, and shall call his name Immanuel"* (Isa 7:14).

Not only does this promise expand upon the concept of woman's seed, but it now introduces the idea that the *"seed"* would not have human paternal parentage. His name *"Immanuel"* means *God is with us* and as this prophecy unfolds in the New Testament we listen in to the Angel speaking to Mary who has just questioned how she could have a child when she had no relations with a man: *"The Holy Ghost shall come upon thee, and the power of the Highest shall overshadow thee: therefore also that holy thing which shall be born of thee shall be called the Son of God."*

It was now clarified how the *"seed of woman"* could crush Satan's head, His father is the Almighty God. God would make a man in His image and likeness by parenting a son born of woman. Here the DNA of God would mingle with human DNA and produce a God-Man in the image and likeness of God.

Isaiah continued his prophecy of the virgin born child as he expanded His name, character, and position:

> *For unto us a child is born, unto us a son is given: and the government shall be upon his shoulder: and his name shall be called Wonderful, Counsellor, The mighty God, The everlasting Father, The Prince of Peace. Of the increase of his government and peace there shall be no end, upon the throne of David, and upon his kingdom, to order it, and to establish it with judgment and with justice from henceforth even for ever. The zeal of the LORD of hosts will perform this* (Isaiah 9:6-7).

Isaiah's prophesy then takes a strange twist as he continued the saga of the coming child portrayed above as Wonderful, Counsellor the Mighty God—a prince and ruler.

> *He is despised and rejected of men; a man of sorrows, and acquainted with grief: and we hid as it were our faces from him; he was despised, and we esteemed him not. Surely he hath borne our griefs, and carried our sorrows: yet we did esteem him stricken, smitten of God, and afflicted. But he was wounded for our transgressions, he was bruised for our iniquities: the chastisement of our peace was upon him; and with his stripes we are healed. All we like sheep*

have gone astray; we have turned every one to his own way; and the LORD hath laid on him the iniquity of us all. He was oppressed, and he was afflicted, yet he opened not his mouth: he is brought as a lamb to the slaughter, and as a sheep before her shearers is dumb, so he openeth not his mouth. He was taken from prison and from judgment: and who shall declare his generation? for he was cut off out of the land of the living: for the transgression of my people was he stricken. And he made his grave with the wicked, and with the rich in his death; because he had done no violence, neither was any deceit in his mouth.

Yet it pleased the LORD to bruise him; he hath put him to grief: when thou shalt make his soul an offering for sin, he shall see his seed, he shall prolong his days, and the pleasure of the LORD shall prosper in his hand. He shall see of the travail of his soul, and shall be satisfied: by his knowledge shall my righteous servant justify many; for he shall bear their iniquities (Isaiah 53:2-11).

Daniel introduced this same Prince (Daniel 9:25-26) who would be cut off for others by the term Messiah which means the *anointed* of God. Anointed as Prince and King—consecrated to make His soul an offering for sin.

Abraham soul rending experience on Mount Moriah now made sense. He had raised his hand with the sharp boning knife ready to plunge it into the body of his son—his only son . . . *"Abraham, Abraham, lay not thine hand upon the lad, neither do thou any thing unto him: for now I know that thou fearest God, seeing thou hast not withheld thy son, thine only son from me."*

Just moments before as he was tying the lad on the wood, he had asked, *"Father . . . Behold the fire and the wood: but where is the lamb for a burnt offering?"* And the old man of faith had responded. *"My son, God will provide himself a lamb for a burnt offering."*

I say, Isaiah's prophecy of a suffering savior making his soul an offering for sins along with Daniel's comment that he would be cutoff, but not for himself— now gave substance and meaning to the awesome scene from Mount Moriah. Abraham's greatest test of faith now prefigured Mount Calvary where God provided *"himself"* a lamb—His only begotten son—and slew Him, the Lamb of God to take away the sin of the world.

The Development of Educational Themes

As God began to unveil His plan to transform fallen sons of Adam into the *image* and *likeness* of Himself, He also launched the greatest educational plan the world has ever seen. In Chapter Two we observed how man became totally controlled by his Psychological Ego-desire System, his Biological Drive System, and a Demonic Mind. His sin had separated him from God— this was his spiritual death. The very concept of God had been erased from his demon controlled mind, and shackled by ego-desires and drives he had no concept of sin and righteousness.

There is an old legend of a valley of blindness where all the inhabitants had lost their physical eyesight. The valley was hemmed in by sheer mountain cliffs jutting upward toward the heavens with no escape route. For generation to generation babies were born without eyes into families who had no words for light, dark, colors, clouds, or towering mountains. Instead they had words that described objects they could touch, or hear, or taste, or smell.

They would go to the rocks that hemmed in their valley—touching them, feeling them, and finding no way to escape the valley they would declare, "This is the end of the world." They would go to the springs in the floor of the valley where water bubbled up and ran away in streams. They would run their fingers and toes through these springs—it seemed to be the only thing coming into this valley. They also felt the tiny water bugs and swimming creatures that surely must be entering their valley through these springs.

Sitting, and thinking, and pondering they would ask, "Do you suppose many, many, years ago we also bubbled up through these springs as tiny water creatures? Is it possible that we have adapted to live outside the water? It must be so—its the only way into our world!

Dear reader, this was not a legend of a valley, it's the story of our world. Man did lose the eyesight for his soul, and hence developed his view of his world by the remaining senses of his physical, psychological, and demonic mind.

This story of the Valley of Blindness illustrates the problem faced by God when He attempted to communicate His plan for man's transformation. Hence, he began to develop mental pictures and symbols of what He would do. These mental pictures began to communicate certain themes by which they could develop concepts of what God was going to do.

I mentioned a moment ago that God launched the greatest educational plan the world has ever seen. First, He developed basic concepts of God, time, man, and matter. By these man could interpret reality. Then God introduced basic precepts to teach man behavior that was acceptable and behavior that was non-acceptable for man in the *image* and *likeness* of God.

Blood. An early theme that God began to develop was that blood—the very essence of life, was the payment for sin. Blood was first shed in the Garden of Eden to provide clothes of skins to cover naked Adam and Eve. Abel knew the kind of offering acceptable by God. After the cleansing of the earth through the flood, God commanded Noah and his sons, "*Whoso sheddeth man's blood, by man shall his blood be shed: for in the image of God made he man*" (Genesis 9:6).

As the Passover lamb was first killed and the lintel and side posts of the doorway were painted with its blood the symbol began to take on greater meaning. As the laws were given at Sinai and the offerings defined they would lay their hands on the head of the offering confessing their sins while the animal was killed and his blood presented unto God.

Sustitutionary Sacrifice. Not only was blood the payment for sins but the blood of a substitutionary sacrifice was necessary for our redemption before God. Hence, the understanding of sin, guilt, sacrifice, and redemption for sins were all part of their spiritual formation provided by God.

Sin and Righteousness. The law with its five defined offerings provided detailed lessons of actions that were not acceptable behavior, and actions that were acceptable behavior before God. Hence, the concepts of sin and righteousness were developed in the minds of Old Israel. These offerings were different for the kinds of sins committed. There were offerings for sins of ignorance, sins committed by accident, sins against persons and sins against property. However, there was no offering for intentional, willful sin.

God's purpose for all of these laws was to teach His people to *"Sanctify yourselves therefore, and be ye holy: for I am the LORD your God"* (Leviticus 20:7).

Guilt. With the laws, the offerings, and even God's punishment for offenders the concept of personal guilt and the understanding that the soul that sinneth it shall die became a major theme concerning which Paul summarized in his letter to the Galatians, *"the law was our schoolmaster to bring us unto Christ, that we might be justified by faith"* (Galatians 3:24).

Faith. The first great lesson of faith was the half-century schooling of Abraham as he journeyed from Ur and throughout Canaan and Egypt waiting for God's promise. It was expanded in the wilderness wanderings of Israel as He led them, and fed them, and punished them, protected them and taught them that they were totally dependent upon Jehovah.

As the Old Testament prophets looked far into the future and foretold both judgments for their failings and God's forgiveness and blessings, it was always with the understanding that future hope was dependent upon faithfulness to God and faith in God's provisions.

As the themes of man's sin and God's provision for sin enlarged, and the prophets painted a verbal picture of the coming kinsman-redeemer—His purpose, His lineage, His birthplace, His character, His conduct, His death and His Kingship, the themes blended to declare that God's provision for human sin was complete. God's redemption draweth nigh!

One Final Thought

Although there were more themes and prophecies concerning God's plan to reclaim man in His *Image* and *Likeness,* the vital thing for us to consider how carefully and completely God unveiled His plan to man.

He provided a way to redeem man, transform man, and yet not force him; but rather He provided a way for man to choose the *Tree of Life* or the *Tree of Death.* If man is truly in the image of God he must have a will to choose.

Jesus expressed it best when He declared, *"I am the way, the truth, and the life: no man cometh unto the Father, but by me"* (John 14:6). He is God's provision to transform the children of Adam into the *image* and *likeness* of God—fulfilling God's ultimate intent.

The Old Testament saint looked forward in faith to accept the substitutionary sacrifice—the Lamb of

> **The Old Testament saints looked forward in faith to accept the substitutionary sacrifice—the Lamb of God—their Messiah. The New Testament believer looks backward and by faith accepts Jesus Christ who died their death that they might live His life.**

God—their Messiah. The New Testament believer looks backward and by faith accepts Jesus Christ who died their death that they might live His life.

Just think what must have happened in heaven at the manger birth of Jesus. Angels had watched and waited while God unveiled His plan for man. They had listened as Mary was told that she would give birth to the Son of God. As the star blazed and the angel chorus announced Messiah's birth—surely the heavens exploded—reverberating with shouts and songs of Angel's praise! For the very first time the ultimate intent of God had been realized—there in the manger was the very first man in the *image* and *likeness* of sovereign God.

And she brought forth her firstborn son, and wrapped him in swaddling clothes, and laid him in a manger; because there was no room for them in the inn.

And there were in the same country shepherds abiding in the field, keeping watch over their flock by night.

And, lo, the angel of the Lord came upon them, and the glory of the Lord shone round about them: and they were sore afraid.

And the angel said unto them, Fear not: for, behold, I bring you good tidings of great joy, which shall be to all people. For unto you is born this day in the city of David a Saviour, which is Christ the Lord.

And this shall be a sign unto you; Ye shall find the babe wrapped in swaddling clothes, lying in a manger.

And suddenly there was with the angel a multitude of the heavenly host praising God, and saying,
Glory to God in the highest, and on earth peace, good will toward men.

Luke 2:7-14

Lesson Four
COMMUNICATING WITH MAN

When God gave man over to a reprobate mind and placed man under the control of his psychological ego-desire system, his biological drive system, and a demonic mind, man lost his spiritual vision. Descending into his *valley of blindness* man became a strict materialist experientially. His entire reality system by which he would interpret all knowledge was now vested in empirical evidence.

Although man had vast resources of the mind and nearly unlimited potential for scientific discoveries and inventions, he could never discover truth of the paranormal. Hence, he could only speculate concerning any reality outside of time, and outside of the physical. These boundaries limited the formation of reality concepts, the development of his language, his philosophy, his value assessments, his precepts, and eventually all of his behavior. Any understandings concerning moral principles, ethical behavior, or virtuous character were totally without foundational standards.

The pre-flood experiment certainly proved this fatal flaw of man's nature. God's analysis of man demonstrated the downward spiral of his conduct: *"And GOD saw that the wickedness of man was great in the earth, and that every imagination of the thoughts of his heart was only evil continually. And it repented the LORD that he had made man on the earth, and it grieved him at his heart"* (Genesis 6:5-6).

Since we have already seen that God had a plan for man's redemption and perfection, we now await the response to the question: How will God communicate with man and reveal truth and knowledge that man cannot—is totally incapable of discovering for himself?

Revelation

The method God established to communicate paranormal truth to man was revelation. *Revelation* is the act of God communicating truth to man that he was incapable of discovering for himself.

> *Revelation* is the act of God communicating truth to man that man is incapable of discovering for himself.

However, there were other problems, man was not only incapable of discovering this Truth, but his language was incapable of expressing this knowledge, and man's mind was also incapable of comprehending it. God had to communicate His truth through the frail concepts of man's limited knowledge in symbols, pictures, and types that man did understand. He had to accommodate this unknown knowledge in terms of the known, and even eventually to change the understandings and knowledge processing of the mind of man.

This was indeed the greatest educational challenge the world has ever witnessed.

Oral Expression and the Written Record

God's communication with man began with oral expression. God spoke and revealed to him truth that man could not discover. The broad term *spiritual,* identifying all that was outside and beyond the physical, may be used to characterize this type of knowledge. The writer of Hebrews in the New Testament looking back over the history of God's processes of revelation described it this way. "*God, who at sundry times and in divers manners spake in time past unto the fathers by the prophet, hath in these last days spoken unto us by his Son . . . .*" (Hebrews 1:1-2). The Greek word translated "*sundry times*" refers to many pieces or portions, and the term "*divers manners*" means different methods and forms. It tells us that God has spoken in times past in many different times and on many different subjects through different methods and forms. God, spake, and spake, and spake again, in dreams, visions, through thunders, voices, physical writing, and even a donkey. The term "*hath spoken*" is a summary conclusion, the God that spake, and spake, and spake has now spoken in His Son.

There is however a step between the oft speaking of history and the final conclusion concerning God's process of revelation. Following the victory over Amalek God commanded Moses "*Write this for a memorial in a book, and rehearse it in the ears of Joshua: for I will utterly put out the remembrance of Amalek from under heaven*" (Exodus 17:14). This began the constant procedure, which God commanded in many future instances, of keeping a permanent written record of God's revelation. Scripture became the descriptive term to identify this permanent record, and scribes were appointed to record and make copies of *The Word of God.* Hence, the oral revelation, the written revelation, and finally the human son of God, who revealed the very image and likeness of God, were all named and described as THE WORD OF GOD.

The Process of Revelation

Paul explained the source and process of revelation to young Timothy with these words. *"All scripture is given by inspiration of God, and is profitable for doctrine, for reproof, for correction, for instruction in righteousness: That the man of God may be perfect, throughly furnished unto all good works"* (2 Timothy 3:16-17).

Peter also addressed this same subject to explain the source and process of God's revelation: *"We have also a more sure word of prophecy . . . . Knowing this first, that no prophecy of the scripture is of any private interpretation. For the prophecy came not in old time by the will of man: but holy men of God spake as they were moved by the Holy Ghost"* (2 Peter 1:19-21).

The word Paul used to describe the process of revelation was *"inspiration of God."* This literally means it was *God breathed.* Paul is also careful to identify the body of God's revelation as *"all Scripture"*.

Peter, referring to the validity of the revelation from God described it as a *"more sure word"* since holy men of God *spake* as they were *moved* by the Holy Ghost. This is the same Spirit of God that had brooded over earth's creation, He is now presented as the one who *"moved"* the holy men of God as they dispensed God's revelation. The word "moved" means *borne* or *carried along.* Their total dependency in prophetic utterance was the Spirit of God.

The Purpose for Revelation

God's purpose for revelation was first to provide a textbook for man to learn and comprehend God's part and man's part in man's spiritual formation which will result in the transformation of a child of Adam into the *image* and *likeness* of God—a son or daughter of sovereign God.

We read Paul's statement to Timothy in the last section where after he identified the source and authority of Scripture, he then stated that it was profitable for doctrine, for reproof, for correction and instruction in righteousness. Paul is here identifying many of the steps and stages of Spiritual Formation. From this catalog of profitable applications of the Word of God we can see a curriculum of instruction. First, the Bible presents doctrine. Doctrine is the basis for our instruction and our learning. These are the bodies of truth that make up our worldview and our system of beliefs. They contain both concepts of what we believe and precepts defining acceptable behavior and nonacceptable behavior. Doctrines will fashion our value system, our interpretive system, and our authority system. These we will discuss in a later lesson.

Secondly, the Bible is profitable for *reproof* and *correction.* Reproof is to point out our errors and provide a basis for conviction. Correction provides the basis and trackage for profitable change of behavior.

Instruction in righteousness is our curriculum for Spiritual Formation in our character development that we might be transformed into the *likeness* of God's first begotten son, Jesus Christ.

The Product of Revelation

Paul continued after he had validated the purpose for biblical revelation and provided an objective for the instruction and direction presented in the Word of God. This teaching/learning objective was *that the man of God may be perfect, throughly furnished unto all good works.*

This teaching/learning objective is divided into two parts. First, it describes the growth and development of the person, and secondly, addresses the achievement of the person. The word translated *perfect* means *complete,* or fully *mature.* The words translated *throughly furnished* has the connotation, one totally equipped for his given task or work.

> **This teaching/learning objective was *that the man of God may be perfect, throughly furnished unto all good works. Throughly furnished* has the connotation, one totally equipped for his given task or work.**

Think back to creation as God declared, *"Let us make man in our image, after our likeness: and let him have dominion . . . ."* Although the fall of man into sin seemed to blast that high intent, God fashioned a plan to provide a payment for man's sin through procreation with the human race. Thus God would become man—a sinless man, that could shed his blood and die for man's sin, so that *"as many as received him, to them gave he power to become the sons of God . . ."* Hence, through the spiritual transformation of man and the instruction furnished through God's revelation, and the teaching and spiritual formation of God's Spirit of holiness, man will truly become the *image* and *likeness* of God.

And even while yet on this earth our God breathed curriculum for spiritual formation can thoroughly equip us to fully achieve the vocation which we are designed by God to achieve. This is even the first step in the recovery of the position of *dominion.*

The Person of Revelation

John introduces his gospel with a bright light piercing earth's darkness reminiscent of the first day of creation.

> *In the beginning was the Word, and the Word was with God, and the Word was God. The same was in the beginning with God. All things were made by him; and without him was not any thing made that was made. In him was life; and the life was the light of men . . . . And the Word was made flesh, and dwelt among us, (and we beheld his glory, the glory as of the only begotten of the Father,) full of grace and truth* (John 1:1-4; 14).

We recall the three pictures of God presented in the first two chapters of Genesis. John now takes us back to the beginning and enlarges the concept of the LORD God of Genesis 2. We spoke of this in the first chapter as Elohiym-Jehovah personal God. We saw God, thus described, form Adam from a little pinch of dust from the earth, and then bend low until lips of omnipotence tough lips of clay and He breathes a puff of breath into Adam's nose and man became a living soul.

John now equates that personage of God with the Word of God—the Son of God, the one who now brought light into a dark world. *Logos* is the Greek word for "*Word*" in this passage. A "word" is the vehicle of communication by which we convey our thoughts, express our feelings, reveal our will, issue commands, and provide instruction. As the Word of God, Jesus Christ was not only the messenger from God, He was the *message* of God. Or as we read earlier from Hebrews, He is God's summary conclusion of God's communication to man—God's last Word to man.

We also need to see what this Word communicated concerning Adam's sinful race and the transformed man now presented as the fulfillment of God's ultimate intent for man. Paul presents this in his letter to the church in Corinth as he wrote to them about the resurrection.

> *And so it is written, The first man Adam was made a living soul; the last Adam was made a quickening spirit. Howbeit that was not first which is spiritual, but that which is natural; and afterward that which is spiritual. The first man is of the earth, earthy: the second man is the Lord from heaven. As is the earthy, such are they also that are earthy: and as is the heavenly, such are they also that are heavenly. And as we have borne the image of the earthy, we shall also bear the image of the heavenly. Now this I say, brethren, that flesh and blood cannot inherit the kingdom of God; neither doth corruption inherit incorruption. Behold, I shew you a mystery; We shall not all sleep, but we shall all be changed, In a moment, in the twinkling of an eye, at the last trump: for the trumpet shall sound, and the dead shall be raised incorruptible, and we shall be changed* (1 Cor 15:45-52).

Notice the language of the first Adam and the last Adam. God breathed and the first Adam became a living soul. The last Adam was made a life-giving spirit. Ponder this carefully. Jesus was the last Adam and in his death for every member of Adam's race took them to death. He

---

Ponder this carefully. Jesus was the last Adam and in his death for every member of Adam's race took us to death!   But in His resurrection he became the Second Man—Headman of a new race—SONS OF GOD!

was sinless and death had no hold on him, but he lay down his life as a substitutionary *Lamb of God*, to take away the sin of the world. But in His resurrection he became the Second Man—Headman of a new race—SONS OF GOD!

That old race were living souls, this new race are spirit beings quickened by the resurrected Christ. That old race bore the image of the earthly Adam; this new race bears the **image** of the eternal God. That old race sinned and in Adam all died; but members of this new race have been conformed to the likeness and character of the First Begotten of the Father. Now robed in their new bodies, like the resurrected body of Jesus Christ, they stand before God in the **image** and **likeness** of their Father. His ultimate intent has finally been achieved!

Postscriptum

We have now been exposed to a brief overview of the *big picture* of what God plans for man, and how He intends to transform individuals from Adam's sinful race to a new race of Sons of God.

We will now go back and study the step by step process of spiritual formation by which we can be transformed into the *image* and then the *likeness* of God. The focus of this study will change from a global view to converge on the individual. It will feature the pre-salvation work of the Spirit of God in both circumstantial rearrangement and mental processing to draw us to Christ. We will study what God does and what we must do in the step by step development for our justification, sanctification and glorification. Each of these developmental steps of growth and development, following our acceptance of Christ, are the elements of Spiritual Formation fulfilling God's Ultimate Intent that we become mature sons and daughters in His Image and Likeness.

"I am the way, the truth, and the life:

no man cometh unto the Father, but by me."

John 14:6

"No man can come to me, except the Father, which hath sent me, draw him . . . "

John 6:44

Lesson Five
LADDER TO GOD

How does a person approach God? This seems like a simple question until we remember the results of the fall of man. Man lost his contact with God and the spiritual environment, he lost his mental concept of God, he became controlled by his psychological ego-desire system, his biological drive system, and a demonic mind.

Even as God began His communication with man, as we studied in the last chapter, He could not have direct communication with man. Man had lost his ability to receive such communication. He was not only man in the valley of blindness—he was also man without ears. Jesus spoke of this inability of man as he recited the only way man could approach God: *"I am the way, the truth, and the life: no man cometh unto the Father, but by me"* (John 14:6). He then complicated this approach even further, *"No man can come to me, except the Father which hath sent me draw him . . . "* (John 6:44).

It is extremely clear from Jesus words that He is the only way to approach God, but even with a way of approach, man is helpless to enter *"the way"* without the drawing power of God. It is also interesting that the words translated *"draw him"* literally means *"to drag."*

Even though God had a plan for man's salvation, He could not communicate directly with man because man was without receiving and decoding instruments to comprehend what God was communicating.

Hence, God had to accommodate himself to man's limitations and enter man's own arena of communication vehicles. He took huge spiritual concepts and translated them by bits and pieces through man's frail words and limited understanding. We know how difficult it is to communicate with infants and small children. We have to speak "baby talk." Thus God used man's "baby talk" language supported by pictures and symbols, and little by little communicated gigantic spiritual concepts into the human "baby talk" so that man could at least get a frail understanding of that concept.

I have spent many enjoyable hours with friends who have spent decades translating a couple books of the Bible into a primitive language. It is a laborious task to find the exact words, tones, and symbols to make the translation comprehendible. How much greater the task of translating God's total Truth into a world of man who have no concept of God, good, and even sin.

With the limitations of man to comprehend spiritual reality well understood, and with the knowledge that God has communicated a plan for man to approach Him, we will now address the question: **How does a man approach God?**

The First Step

We have a list of six theological words that all deal with some step in man's approach to God, but which is the first step?

Repentance, Conviction, Sanctification, Illumination, Revelation, Justification

We will use the symbol of a ladder to illustrate the step by step process of approaching God. In the last chapter we were introduced to *Revelation,* which was defined as *the act of God communicating truth to man that he was incapable of discovering for himself.* We also learned that the Bible was the complete revelation of this truth and introduced the living Word.

It is only by contact with the Word of God that man can know anything of God. This contact may be by reading the Word, hearing the Word, hearing only a concept of the Word in a song, tract, or even a paraphrase. In some way man must come in contact with the Bible, the Word of God. Hence, the very first step in man's approach to God is hearing the Word of God. *"Faith cometh by hearing, and hearing by the word of God"* (Romans 10:17). And furthermore we know, *"But without faith it is impossible to please him: for he that cometh to God must believe that he is, and that he is a rewarder of them that diligently seek him"* (Hebrews 11:6).

This reality accentuates the need to preach the Word, proclaim the Word, present the Word to others, it is the Word that giveth life. Contact with the Word—God's revelation of reality—is the very first vital step by which a person begins his approach to God.

The Second Step

The second step which should be taken immediately following the first step is *illumination.* Illumination is the work of the Spirit of God causing a

> **Illumination is the work of the Spirit of God causing a person to comprehend God's revealed Truth.**

person to comprehend God's revelation. Illuminate literally means to turn on a light. The Spirit of God enlightens the dark recesses of the mind of a person to cause him to see and understand truth.

Just suppose a non-Christian read from Matthew 11:28 as Jesus presented this invitation, "*Come unto me, all ye that labour and are heavy laden, and I will give you rest.*" At that very moment the Spirit of God causes the person to remember his burden of difficulties; He understands that he needs help, he understands the promise of rest. All of this is the work of the Spirit illuminating his mind.

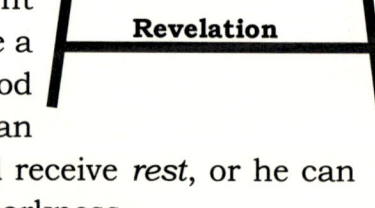

This is a strategic moment because the person has to make a choice. His mind has understood but his will has to respond. He can say yes to Jesus' invitation and receive *rest,* or he can say no and go out into greater darkness.

If he responds in the positive, he advances to the next step on the ladder of approach to God.

The Third Step

Conviction is the third step in our approach to God. This, again, is another work of the Spirit of God causing a person to personalize his guilt. Suppose a person has just read or heard Romans 3:23, "*For all have sinned, and come short of the glory of God.*" First, the Spirit of God turns his light on the concept of sin, and that sin causes displeasure with God. The person begins to think of all the sinful deeds he has seen and heard around him. Suddenly there is that awful pang of guilt as he cries, "I have sinned, I have come short of the glory of God— I am guilty!" Then suppose at that very moment his attention is directed to another verse of Scripture, Romans 6:23, "*For the wages of sin is death; but the gift of God is eternal life through Jesus Christ our Lord.*"

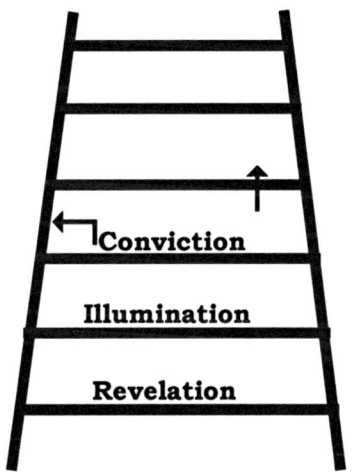

"I have sinned, I am facing death—I need this gift,

Convicion is the work of the Spirit of God causing a person to personalize guilt.

---

dear God . . ." This is the operation of conviction produced by the Spirit of God brooding over a human soul much like He brooded over the chaos in the precreation world.

The guilty soul, however again faces a moment of choice. He has been illuminated to comprehend God's Word; He has been convicted to personalize his guilt, but his will must choose. If he responds to God's invitation to receive His gift of eternal life, he will move on to the next step of repentance. But if he resists the drawing of the Spirit, he will harden his heart as Pharaoh of old and turn away from his approach to God.

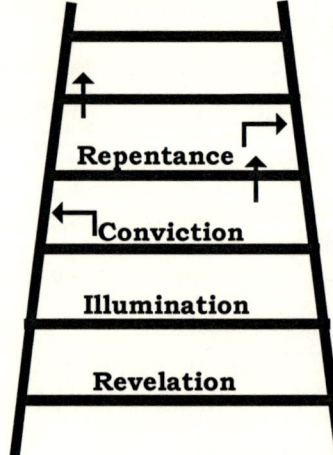

The Fourth Step

The fourth step on our ladder of approach to God is the step of repentance. We think of repentance as being sorry for our sin and it is, but it literally means *to change our mind.* When Jesus began his earthly ministry he began (Matthew 4:17) by commanding : *"Repent, for the kingdom of heaven is at hand."* He was crying, "change your way of thinking, change from man's conclusions to God's assertions." This again is a choice of will for it is an act of faith accepting God's revelation as truth and acting on it. Once again a person can turn away from repentance. The writer of Hebrews presents the truth of this fearsome moment: (Hebrews 6:4-6) *"For it is impossible for those who were once enlightened, and have tasted of the heavenly gift, and were made partakers of the Holy Ghost, And have tasted the good word of God, and the powers of the world to come, If they shall fall away, to renew them again unto repentance . . . ."*

Read and ponder this carefully. These steps of approach to God are each a labor of the Spirit of God drawing, assisting, enabling a person to come to God. He is doing the work Jesus promised, *"for he shall receive of mine, and shall shew it unto you."* If, however, a person who has been enlightened, has tasted of the heavenly gift, has been a partaker of the drawing work of the Spirit—but turns away. He cannot by himself bring himself back to repentance. But if by faith he reaches out toward Jesus, who declared *"For God so loved the world, that he gave his only begotten Son, that whosoever believeth in him should not perish, but have everlasting life."* If by faith he embraces Jesus as his personal savior he will have taken the final step in his approach to God. It is the final step in our approach to God since John 1:12 declares: *"But as many as received him, to them gave he power to become the sons of God, even to them that believe on his name."*

The Fifth Step

This step results in our justification and spiritual conception. Justification means that God has accepted Jesus death as payment for my sin and declared that I am righteous. My state of righteousness in Christ is *just-as-if-I'd* never sinned. When we embrace Jesus Christ as our savior the Spirit of God conceives a child of God in our spirit being—in the image of our

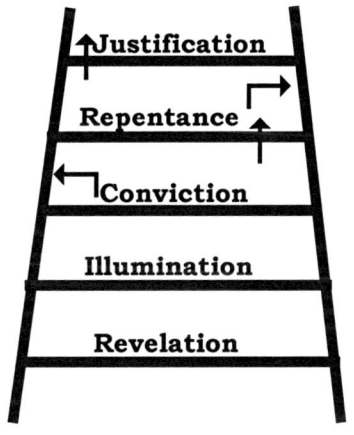

Father. We speak of this as new birth, or being born from above. It is a literal conception and John declares (1 John 3:9-10) that God's seed remains in us because we are born (conceived) of God. In that moment the demonic mind is replaced by the mind of Christ.

Paul summarized this tremendous reality in Romans 5:1: *"Therefore being justified by faith, we have peace with God through our Lord Jesus Christ."* Our approach to God is complete—we are at peace.

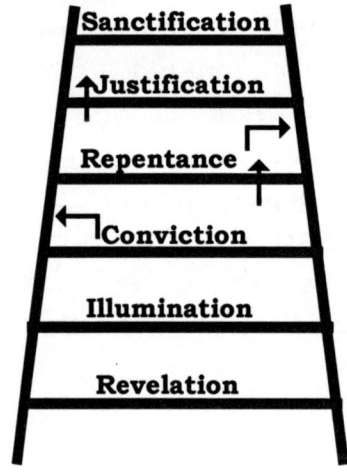

Growing Up Into Christ

As sons and daughters of sovereign God we are now to grow up into the likeness of Jesus. Our spiritual conception ensures that we are in the *image* of our Father and now we will be perfected into His *likeness*. We will represent this by another step on our ladder. It is not a step of approach to God but a step in becoming like our father.

This step will be known as *sanctification*. Sanctification means "set apart" and it involves the process of controlling both our psychological ego-desire system and our biological drive system by the mind of Christ being structured in us to set us apart from sin and set apart unto God. This is the developmental process of being transformed by the renewing of our mind as expressed in Romans 12:2. This transformation is the metamorphosis similar to the ugly crawling caterpillar being transformed into the brilliant, beautiful butterfly. We are transformed from the old ugly worm of Adam's race to the *likeness* of God.

This is also the work of the Spirit of God teaching, drawing, brooding over us. Jesus said when he foretold the coming of Spirit, *"when he, the Spirit of truth, is come, he will guide you into all truth: for he shall not speak of himself; but whatsoever he shall hear, that shall he speak: and he will shew you things to come. He shall glorify me: for he shall receive of mine, and shall shew it unto you."*

It is also the work delegated to the Spirit of Holiness by the Father in Romans 8:26-29:

> *Likewise the Spirit also helpeth our infirmities: for we know not what we should pray for as we ought: but the Spirit itself maketh intercession for us with groanings which cannot be uttered. And he that searcheth the hearts knoweth what is the mind of the Spirit, because he maketh intercession for the saints according to the will of God. And we know that all things work together for good to them that love God, to them who are the called according to his purpose. For whom he did foreknow, he also did predestinate to be conformed to the image of his Son, that he might be the firstborn among many brethren.*

The word translated *image* in verse 29 is the Greek equivalent of the Hebrew word *likeness*. God is transforming us into the likeness—the character of Jesus.

We used the symbol of a ladder to illustrate the step by step approach to God for our justification. Now it is important to recognize that when one has been justified and conceived into new life by the Spirit of God that now we have access through Christ by one Spirit unto the Father (Ephesians 2:18). However, as we grow and develop in our sanctification, we will retrace the same steps as we did in our first approach. It is still the Word of God that *reveals* spiritual truth we cannot discover for ourselves. We must have the *illumination* of the Spirit to enable us to comprehend God's Word. We will be *convicted* of our weaknesses and our need, and we

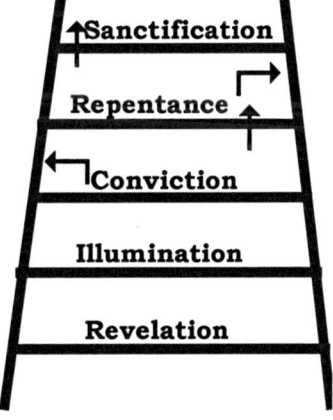

will be challenged to *change our mind* from our own
opinions and conclusions to God's directives. These are
the steps of spiritual formation to achieve our complete
sanctification.

In our approach to God we became new creatures
in Christ through Spiritual conception. We became a son
or daughter of sovereign God in the womb of the old
Adam person. For the remainder of our earthly existence
God desires that we grow-up like His first begotten son
so that when we receive our glorified bodies in our
heavenly home, we will be fully mature sons and
daughters of sovereign God. This is why he has given us
an approach to Himself. The first approach to God is for
our sonship and then our daily approach to God through
the study of His Word is for our sanctification. Hence,
we are procreated in the *image of God* by our Spiritual
conception and we are transformed into *His holy likeness*
by the renewing of our mind and obedience to His will.

Lesson Six
GOD BECAME FLESH

The first hint that God's plan to make man in His image and likeness entailed procreation with the human race of Adam was concealed within the curse upon the serpent. "I *will put enmity between thee and the woman, and between thy seed and her seed; it shall bruise thy head, and thou shalt bruise his heel*" (Genesis 3:15). Here the seed of woman is described as one who would *break* or *overwhelm* Satan. Hence, the hint that this one would be man—but greater than Adam-man!

We have already discussed the prophecies of Isaiah which declared that "*a virgin shall conceive, and bear a son, and shall call his name Immanuel.*" This seed of woman is called Immanuel—which literally means *"with us is God."* Isaiah later expanded this concept by declaring His name, "*Wonderful, Counsellor, The mighty God, The everlasting Father, The Prince of Peace.*" There can remain no doubt that a woman conceives, without human sperm, and gives birth to One who is God.

As John picked up his pen to describe one with whom he had a close earthly friendship, he described Him as the offspring of God. "*And the Word was made flesh, and dwelt among us, (and we beheld his glory, the glory as of the only begotten of the Father,) full of grace and truth*" (John 1:14).

If there was any remaining doubt of the nature of this One which was named Jesus, then the angel's response to Mary, when she questioned how she could conceive without a man impregnating her, certainly blasts those doubts.

> *And the angel answered and said unto her, The Holy Ghost shall come upon thee, and the power of the Highest shall overshadow thee: therefore also that holy thing which shall be born of thee shall be called the Son of God* (Luke 1:35).

There can also be no doubt concerning the nature of Jesus. We know that human babies have 23 chromosomes from the mother and 23 chromosomes from the father each laden with genes. Hence, Jesus was endowed with genes—human and divine, which are the functional units of inheritance.

> **Jesus was one being, but with two natures—fully God and fully man. He was the fulfillment of the ultimate intent of God—Man, in our *image* after our *likeness*.**

He was one being, but with two natures-—fully God and fully man. He was the fulfillment of the ultimate intent of God—Man, in our *image* after our *likeness*.

The Condescension of the Son of God

We cannot totally express that which we do not totally comprehend. Paul speaks of things we cannot fully know, as mysteries. In some mysterious way the Son of God, who was present with the Father before the world was, (John 17:5) laid aside His Glory and became man. It was a voluntary choice as we hear him whisper in Psalms 40:7-8 *"Lo, I come: in the volume of the book it is written of me, I delight to do thy will, O my God: yea, thy law is within my heart."*

This will of God caused him to divest himself of heavenly glory and become flesh. As a Man he walked the dusty paths of earth where his humanity was in full relief. As a child He was dependent on others, subject to His parents, subject to the Law. As a man he became weary, was hungry, thirsty, and wept. As God he knew men's thoughts, He could command demons, heal sickness, reprehend nature, raise the dead.

Paul described His condensation and humiliation as an example for our compliance.

> *Let this mind be in you, which was also in Christ Jesus: Who, being in the form of God, thought it not robbery to be equal with God: But made himself of no reputation, and took upon him the form of a servant, and was made in the likeness of men: And being found in fashion as a man, he humbled himself, and became obedient unto death, even the death of the cross. Wherefore God also hath highly exalted him, and given him a name which is above every name* (Philippians 2:5-9).

The Temptation of the Son of Man

It was through temptation that Adam and Eve failed, and Jesus *"was in all points tempted like as we are, yet without sin"* (Hebrews 4:15). His temptation was designed as a test of His obedience to His Father much as the Eden temptation of Adam and Eve.

Jesus had just been baptized by John in Jordan. Coming out of the waters the heavens had thundered with a voice declaring, *"This is my beloved Son, in whom I am well pleased."* From this delightful experience Jesus was led by the Spirit into the wilderness where he fasted for forty days and forty nights preparing for an encounter with the devil. As his hunger pangs wrenched His innards, the devil called with the same doubting tone as he had enticed Eve, *"If thou be the Son of God, command that these stones be made bread."* It was a challenge to prove His deity and to satisfy His hunger drive. Eve's temptation was to become like God, Jesus' temptation was to prove Himself God. Both were challenges to human ego, but Jesus' temptation combined desire with drives. Prove yourself to be the Son of God and at the same time satisfy your hunger. The language of the tempter was something like this: "Here you are hungry, cast out, alone, needy, poor, and yet the Son of God. If you truly have this power, how easy could you satisfy your wants." Both Eve and Jesus were challenged to doubt and distrust God's Word.

Jesus responded, *"It is written, Man shall not live by bread alone, but by every word that proceedeth out of the mouth of God."*

Satan then brought Jesus to a pinnacle of the temple and again challenged His claim to deity: *"If thou be the Son of God, cast thyself down: for it is written, 'He shall give his angels charge concerning thee: and in their hands they shall bear thee up, lest at any time thou dash thy foot against a stone."*

Now the temple was surrounded with porches 5o feet broad and 150 feet high. The southern porch was 67 feet broad and 150 feet high. From the top of this to the bottom of the valley was more than 700 feet. Josephus stated that one could scarcely look down without dizziness.

Satan was not only challenging Jesus' to prove His Sonship, but he was challenging Him to demonstrate that He trusted His Father, and that his Father could be trusted. This was a challenge to presumption.

Jesus again referenced Scripture, *"Thou shalt not tempt the Lord thy God."*

Next the devil transported Jesus into a high mountain and shewed Him all the kingdoms of the world in a moment of time. *"All this power will I give thee, and the glory of them, for that is delivered unto me; and to whomsoever I will I give it. If thou therefore wilt worship me, all shall be thine."*

What a powerful appeal to ego-ambition. The global kingdom without a cross, the glory of nations without price—a gift just for bowing down in worship to the prince of this world. This is a bolder attack than the other temptations. They had been based on an appeal to physical needs and ego-desire. They were not violations of God's law nor acts of sin. This was now a proposition that the Son of God worship him which was a direct violation of Scripture—a temptation to idolatry.

Jesus' responses to the first two temptations were simply a refusal based on scripture. Here Jesus invokes His authority and commands Satan by name, *"get thee behind me, Satan!"* He drove him from His presence.

"Get thee behind me, Satan: for it is written, Thou shalt worship the Lord thy God, and him only shalt thou serve."

These were not the only temptations Jesus faced in his earthly journey, but these were a designed attack by Satan to thwart God's plan to rescue Adam's race through Jesus the Christ.

Although Jesus was man and was indeed tempted in every possible way, He did not sin; thus proving that although He was son of man, He also was Son of God.

The Death of the Son of God

The death of Jesus was foreshadowed throughout the Old Testament. To the serpent it was described as the bruising of His heel. To Abraham it was the sacrificial lamb that God would provide, and to the Israelites in Egypt it was the Passover Lamb. Four of the five sacrifices identified in the first five chapters of Leviticus including the burnt offering, the sin offering, the peace offering and the trespass offering, required the death of the sacrificial animal and cleansing by its blood.

Isaiah captured this prophetic meaning in his descriptive utterances in chapter 53: *He is despised and rejected of men; a man of sorrows, and acquainted with grief: and we hid as it were our faces from him; he was despised, and we esteemed him not. Surely he hath borne our griefs, and carried our sorrows: yet we did esteem him stricken, smitten of God, and afflicted. But he was wounded for our transgressions, he was bruised for our iniquities: the chastisement of our peace was upon him; and with his stripes we are healed. All we like sheep have gone astray; we have turned every one to his own way; and the LORD hath laid on him the iniquity of us all. He was oppressed, and he was afflicted, yet he opened not his mouth: he is brought as a lamb to the slaughter, and as a sheep before her shearers is dumb, so he openeth not his mouth.*

The author of Hebrews (2:6-9) quotes from Psalm 8 asking the question, "*What is man, that thou art mindful of him? or the son of man, that thou visitest him?*" He comments to his position a little lower than angels, and that God had placed "all things" in subjection under his feet. Then he remarked that we do not yet see all things placed under him, *"But we see Jesus, who was made a little lower than the angels for the suffering of death. . . ."* Hence, the single purpose for which Jesus entered the human race was to *"taste death for every man."*

Compare this concept to Paul's descriptive title for Jesus in 1 Corinthians 15:45: "t*he last Adam."* Since He came to earth to *"taste death for every man,"* and He died as the "last Adam" that death pronounced finality for Adam's race. It was an accomplished fact when Jesus cried from the cross, "It is finished (John 19:30)," although we do not yet see it finalized in time.

The Exaltation of the Son of God

As Jesus dismissed His spirit on Calvary's cross they took his blessed body that had borne the sins of every child of Adam and placed it in a rock hewn tomb. He had carried the race to death. The only son of man that had never sinned laid down His life—the spotless lamb of God had taken away the sin of the world. Now his lifeless body lay in the cold dank tomb.

Here the Spirit of God was brooding much as we saw him in Genesis 1:2 hovering over the precreation chaos. Peter tells us that *"Christ also hath once suffered for sins, the just for the unjust, that he might bring us to God, being put to death in the flesh, but quickened by the Spirit"* (1 Peter 3:18).

Resurrection through the quickening power of the Spirit of God is much more that just bringing Jesus back to life. But as we saw in a previous lesson (1 Corinthians 15:45) Jesus died as the last Adam a natural living soul, but he was raised as a *new man* a *quickening spirit*—a spiritual being. God had totally achieved his ultimate intent to create man in His *image* and *likeness*. It was not simply one being, but as the "second man" the resurrected Christ would be the head-man of a new race of mankind—spirit beings procreated in the image and likeness of God.

"*God also hath highly exalted him (Jesus Christ) and given him a name that is above every name*" (Philipians 2:9). "*He raised him from the dead, and set him at his own right hand in heavenly places, far above principality, and power, and might, and dominion, and every name that is named, not only in this world, but also in that which is to come*" (Epesians 1:20-21).

The Present Ministry of The Son of God

The God that humbled Himself and became flesh for the purpose of presenting himself as a substitutionary sacrifice to die for the sins of Adam's posterity is now seated at the right hand of His Father awaiting the final destruction of His enemies. In that position, He is mediator and intercessor—"*For there is one God, and one mediator between God and men, the man Christ Jesus*" (1 Timothy 2:5). He is our great high priest in the heavenlies:

> *Seeing then that we have a great high priest, that is passed into the heavens, Jesus the Son of God, let us hold fast our profession. For we have not an high priest which cannot be touched with the feeling of our infirmities; but was in all points tempted like as we are, yet without sin. Let us therefore come boldly unto the throne of grace, that we may obtain mercy, and find grace to help in time of need.* (Hebrews 4:14-16).

And when we sin, it is Jesus, the one who knows, experientially, the bombardment of temptations, seated on the right hand of the Father, that is our advocate. *"My little children, these things write I unto you, that ye sin not. And if any man sin, we have an advocate with the Father, Jesus Christ the righteous"* (1 John 2:1.

To his fearful disciples huddled in the upper room awaiting His crucifixion Jesus gave promises that extend even to us. He reemphasized His promises to hear and answer prayer. He promised that he would not leave them comfortless and promised to send them the Spirit:

> *Even the Spirit of truth; whom the world cannot receive, because it seeth him not, neither knoweth him: but ye know him; for he dwelleth with you, and shall be in you.* And then He declared: *I will not leave you comfortless: **I will come to you***" (John 14:17-18).

Then Jesus summarized the true earthly position of each of His followers: *"At that day ye shall know that I am in my Father, and ye in me, and I in you"*—totally immersed in God.

In the words of the apostle Paul (Ephesians 1:18-19) *"The eyes of your understanding being enlightened; that ye may know what is the hope of his calling, and what the riches of the glory of his inheritance in the saints, And what is the exceeding greatness of his power to usward who believe, according to the working of his mighty power"*—All of this because God became Man.

1 There was a man of the Pharisees named Nicodemus, a ruler of the Jews.

2 This man came to Jesus by night and said to Him, "Rabbi, we know that You are a teacher come from God; for no one can do these signs that You do unless God is with him."

3 Jesus answered and said to him, "Most assuredly, I say to you, unless one *is conceived*[1] from above he cannot see the kingdom of God."

4 Nicodemus said to Him, "How can a man *be conceived* when he is old? Can he enter a second time into his mother's womb ?"

5 Jesus answered, "Most assuredly, I say to you, unless one *is conceived* of water and the Spirit, he cannot enter the kingdom of God.   6 That which *is conceived* of the flesh is flesh, and that which *is conceived* of the Spirit is spirit.   7 Do not marvel that I said to you, 'You must be *conceived* from above.'   8 The wind blows where it wishes, and you hear the sound of it, but cannot tell where it comes from and where it goes. So is everyone who *is conceived* of the Spirit."

John 3:1-5

---

[1]A direct translation of the Greek word "gennao" (ghen-nah'-o); to procreate (properly, of the father, but by extension of the mother); to conceive.

Lesson Seven
CONCEIVED BY GOD

How can we describe a person who declares that he has become a Christian? From physical observation there doesn't seem to be much change. Jesus described the person by pointing to the wind: *"The wind bloweth where it listeth, and thou hearest the sound thereof, but canst not tell whence it cometh, and whither it goeth: so is every one that is born (conceived) of the Spirit"* (John 3:8).

As behavior improves and character changes demonstrating love, joy and peace, we can recognize that inner changes are affecting the outward behavior. Hence, we recognize that becoming a Christian is describing an inward change that causes an outward manifestation.

Paul summarized to the Corinthian church. *"Therefore if any man be in Christ, he is a new creature:*

> . . . becoming a Christian is describing an inward change that causes an outward manifestation.

old things are passed away; behold, all things are become new" (2 Corinthians 5:17). The phrase *"In Christ"* means to be united to Christ by faith; or to be in him as the branch is in the vine so as to derive all its nourishment and support from it—entirely sustained by it. Jesus described this condition: *"Abide in me, and I in you. As the branch cannot bear fruit of itself, except it abide in the vine; no more can ye, except ye abide in me"* (John 15:4).

Hence, the one who is in Christ is a *new creature* or creation, or *new being*. The remainder of this verse has been somewhat distorted by translation into English.

The word "things" referring to "old" and "all things" referencing the "new" have both been inserted by translators to make it more readable in English. This verse does not focus on "things" it focuses on the old being and the new being. A literal translation of the Greek text reads: *"If any man be in Christ, he is a new creation: the old one has passed; behold the new."*

> *"If any man be in Christ, he is a new procreation: the old one has passed—behold the new!"*

What is the New?

In John 3 we have the narrative of Nicodemus' night visit with Jesus. Nicodemus enters professing to know that Jesus had come from God since he had seen His miracles. He was professing to know something of the spiritual realm. Jesus actually contradicted Nicodemus declaring he could "see" or *comprehend* nothing about the kingdom of God except he is "born anew" or "conceived from above."

Nicodemus retorted, proving he comprehended nothing of the spiritual realm, *"How can a man be born (conceived anew) when he is old? Can he enter the second time into his mother's womb and be born?"*

"Jesus answered, Verily verily, I say unto thee, Except a man be born of water and of the Spirit, he cannot enter into the kingdom of God." Bible scholars are divided on the meaning of "born of water." Some believe he was speaking of baptism, and others just of the washing and cleansing power of water both actually and symbolically. Both of these are not historically nor contextually coherent. Jesus explained what he meant in His next

statement. Nicodemus had confused physical birth and spiritual birth, and Jesus in seeking to clarify this confusion compared physical birth and spiritual birth. "Born of water" refers to physical birth as that which resulted in physical human life, and "born of the spirit" as that which results in life in the spiritual realm or the kingdom of God.

This is doubly demonstrated in verse 6 which is a continuation of verse five, as Jesus points out: *"That which is born of flesh, is flesh . . . ."* Physical human birth produces another physical human being. "And that which is born (conceived) of the Spirit, is spirit." With this understanding we recognize that Spirit birth is truly the second birth. "So Nicodemus," Jesus was saying, *"Don't marvel, or don't wonder, that I said unto you, Ye must be born again (conceived from above)."*

Nicodemus, probably shaking his head in near disbelief, questioned, "How can these things be?

Jesus answered after questioning how it could be that a Israeli teacher didn't know about new birth, *"And as Moses lifted up the serpent in the wilderness, even so must the Son of man be lifted up: That whosoever believeth in him should not perish, but have eternal life."*

In this response it is clear that believing in the Son of man was the key for experiencing this second birth. John also expressed this in Chapter one, verse 12: *"But as many as received him (Jesus the Word), to them gave he power to become sons of God, even to them that believe on his name; which were born (conceived), not of blood, nor of the will of the flesh, nor of the will of man, but of God."*

In His discussion with Nicodemus, Jesus had used the phrase, *"Born of the Spirit and Born again."*   The Greek word translated *"born"* was not the word for "birth" but the word for conceived or conception.

In His discussion with Nicodemus, Jesus had used the phrase, *"Born of the Spirit and Born again."* The Greek word translated *"born"* was not the word for "birth" but the word for conceived or conception.

Notice the full lesson presented in this night visit with Nicodemus. When a person embraces Jesus Christ as his personal savior, the Spirit of God conceives within that one a spirit being—in the *image* of God and with the DNA of God.   *"For God so loved the world, that he gave his only begotten Son, that whosoever believeth in him should not perish, but have everlasting life."*

In his epistle John adds to his lesson from the Gospel of John: *"Whosoever is born of God doth not commit sin; for his seed remaineth in him: and he cannot sin, because he is conceived by God* (1 John 3:9). Here also the phrase translated *"born of God"* has the concept of *procreated* or *conceived by God*, and the word for *"seed"* is the Greek word *sperma.*

My spiritual conception produced a new being in my inward parts. It is a spiritual new beginning through which, as a child of God, I have been procreated in the image of my Father. Although I am in the embryonic stage of my new life I am a spirit being, much like Adam and Eve were before their spirit died through disobeying God and eating of the tree of knowledge of good and evil. Not only am I a living spirit being, I have been given a new mind (1 Corinthians 2:16)—the mind of Christ, which will become the control center of my new life. In addition to all this the Spirit of God has been given as Jesus promised His disciples in the upper room: *"And I will pray the Father, and he shall give you another Comforter, that he may abide with you for ever; Even the Spirit of truth; whom the world cannot receive, because it seeth him not, neither knoweth him: but ye know him; for he dwelleth with you, and shall be in you"* (John 14:16-17).

Hence, the Spirit of God which brooded over the pre-creation chaos to bring form out of formlessness, and "brooded over the lifeless body of the dead Jesus in the power of resurrection, now takes up permanent residence in our spirit to "brood" over our lives to produce spiritual formation to conform us to the *likeness* of God.

What is Still Old?

Man was originally created a tri-part being—spirit, soul, and body. Although spirit-death passed on all man after the fall, in spiritual conception a new spirit was procreated within us with an old human soul, and an old physical body. Yet, the purpose of God for His new son or daughter is to sanctify us wholly. *"And the very God of peace sanctify you wholly; and I pray God your whole spirit and soul and body be preserved blameless unto the coming of our Lord Jesus Christ"* (1 Thessalonians 5:23). Thus it is the purpose of God through the new spirit person supported by a new control center of the mind to totally refashion, through spiritual formation, the psychological and biological parts of man to glorify our Father.

> We are a God procreated spirit being, but still have an old human soul, and an old Adam body.

*But we have this treasure in earthen vessels, that the excellency of the power may be of God, and not of us. We are troubled on every side, yet not distressed; we are perplexed, but not in despair;   Persecuted, but not forsaken; cast down, but not destroyed; Always bearing about in the body the dying of the Lord Jesus, that the life also of Jesus might be made manifest in our body. For we which live are alway delivered unto death for Jesus' sake, that the life also of Jesus might be made manifest in our mortal flesh . . . . For which cause we faint not; but though our outward man perish, yet the inward man is renewed day by day (*2 Corrinthians 4:7-10;16).

Hence, we recognize that life on earth for the Christian is like the prenatal development of a physical child in the womb of his mother. Even as the old physical body weakens and wears out through the aging process wrought in it by sin's curse, the inward man, conceived by sovereign God, is being renewed day by day.

Things to Ponder

The word ponder means to weigh in the mind, to reflect upon, to carefully consider quietly, soberly, and deeply. This is the mental scrutiny that we need to give each *carat* of our spirit-being.

Who am I?—Who Are You? These were the questions Moses asked of God beside the burning bush. God responded, "I AM THAT I AM—I am the sovereign self existent God! As a newborn Christian asking "Who am I?" The Biblical response is "you are a spirit conceived son, or daughter, of sovereign God."

As the question, "Who are You, God," is breathed by a new Christian, God lovingly and caringly responds, "I am your Father, you are My child!" This understanding changed my life more than any other teaching in my early Christian life. Living in cattle country I would ride through the pasture reviewing the herds of cattle, and hear the whisper in my soul, "My Father owns the cattle on a thousand hills—I am the son of sovereign God."

I would lie on my back and gaze into the starry heavens—seeing galaxy heaped on galaxy. Again the whisper in my soul, "My Father spoke and the worlds appeared—I am son of sovereign God."

Kill me, some may!
Conquer me—nothing can!
I am the Spirit of God
Fused in the soul of man—
I am son of sovereign God!

Where am I? Jesus speaking to his fearful disciples meeting in the upper room just hours before his death on Calvary desired to give them a sense of protection and security. He had assured them that although He was going away that he would return for them. He promised them the indwelling Spirit., and then, in John 14:20, He unveiled their position of security. *"At that day* (the day the Spirit takes up residency in your heart) *ye shall know that I am in my Father, and ye in me, and I in you."*

Try to draw a symbol of that statement. Use a large circle to represent the Father, and a concentric circle within it to represent Christ. Put a square in the circle to represent each one of us. Then place a "C" within the  square representing the Spirit of Christ. Look at this: God is on our outside, God is on our inside—we are totally immersed in God. No wonder Paul could tell the Corinthians (3:16) *"Know ye not that ye are the temple of God, and that the Spirit of God dwelleth in you?*

> God is on our outside, God is on our inside— we are totally immersed in God.

No wonder our Father declares: *"O Fear thou not; for I am with thee: be not dismayed; for I am thy God: I will strengthen thee; yea, I will help thee; yea, I will uphold thee with the right hand of my righteousness"* (Isaiah 41:10).

Abba Father! As Jesus prayed in the Garden with the spectre of death hanging over him, He cried *Abba Father . . . .* This is the same cry that bursts from our lips when we comprehend our true sonship. Paul wrote of this reality to the Galatian Christians:

> *But when the fulness of the time was come, God sent forth his Son, made of a woman, made under the law, To redeem them that were under the law, that we might receive the adoption of sons. And because ye are sons, God hath sent forth the Spirit of his Son into your hearts, crying, Abba, Father. Wherefore thou art no more a servant, but a son; and if a son, then an heir of God through Christ* (Galatians 4:4-7).

This is a strange cry. *Abba* is the Syriac word for *Father* and then Jesus repeated the word Father in His native language. Hence, He seems to say Father, Father, and the cry that the Spirit of Christ prompts in our hearts is Father, Father. The Syriac translation of this Romans 8:15 reads: "By which we call the Father our Father." God is not only The Father in general, He is my Father— Abba, Father.

We also find Christians who are confused about their spiritual conception and take the Biblical verse about adoption and assume that God has only adopted us from Adam's family to His family. No, no—we that have embraced Jesus Christ as our personal savior have been conceived by God—his child by procreation. I am His true son, but I have not yet received my adoption. We have received the Spirit of adoption (Romans 8:15), but have not received our adoption. Adoption in these references speaks of our inheritance. It is the legal rights of heirship. It corresponds to the Jewish rite of Bar Mitzvah where a son of the father becomes the heir. Before this event the son is of the same status of the servants.

Right now on earth, "The Spirit itself beareth witness with our spirit, that we are the children of God: And if children, then heirs; heirs of God, and joint-heirs with Christ (Romans 8:16-17). Right now we are sons and daughters of sovereign God indwelled with the Spirit of Adoption who causes us to cry "Abba, Father!" The day is quickly approaching when God's trumpet shall sound and we shall be summoned into His presence for our Bar Mitzvah of the heavenlies—heirs of God and joint-heirs with Christ.

Son at the Breakfast Table. Among the blessings of sonship there is a special privilege that I confess changed my entire life when I realized that I was a Spirit conceived son of sovereign God. When Jesus taught His disciples to pray (Luke 11) He instructed them to pray: "Our Father which art in heaven." Prayer is the prerogative of children of God—a family privilege!

Prayer is not coming before some great king or ruler crying, "Please tilt your septre toward me"—No, prayer is coming as a son to the breakfast table, crying, "Father, this is what I need as I go work in your field today."

As Jesus presented His final teachings to His disciples in the upper room in John 14, 15, and 16, He emphasized the privilege and expanded the promises of prayer.

He had given His new commandment that they should love one another as He had loved them. He had quelled there troubled hearts, by stating that He was going to prepare a place for them and would return to take them with Him. In verse 12 He heightened their responsibility by saying: *"He that believeth on me, the works that I do shall he do also; and greater works than these shall he do, because I go unto my father."*

Then Jesus dropped a verbal bomb—*"And whatsoever ye shall ask in my name, that will I do, that the Father may be glorified in the Son, If ye shall ask anything in my name, I will do it." Whatsoever ye shall ask—If ye ask anything . . . .*

Many years ago when I first remember reading this I was nearly overwhelmed by these unlimiting words. Jesus had told His followers that he that believeth on me will do *greater things* than I have done; and now He was promising them the power to do these greater things by *whatsoever* they would request.

I read on to Chapter 15 of the vine and branch relationship, Jesus said (vs. 8): *"I am the vine, you are the branches . . . Herein is my Father glorified, that ye bear much fruit . . . . Ye have not chosen me, but I have chosen you, and ordained you, that ye should go and bring forth fruit, and that your fruit should remain:* **that whatsoever ye shall ask of the Father in my name, he may give it you"** (vs. 16)

In Chapter 14 Jesus used the *whatsoever* word to promise power to do greater things, and in Chapter 15 He repeated it to promise greater productivity. Whatsoever you need to complete My mission—I will give you.

In the next Chapter the scene darkens as threatening persecution runs rampant. They will even kill you thinking they are doing God a service. You will even weep and lament, and have sorrow—but remember *"I will see you again, and your heart will rejoice . . .Verily, verily, I say unto you, Whatsoever ye shall ask the Father in my name, he will give it you. Hitherto have ye asked nothing in my name: Ask, and ye shall receive that your joy shall be full."*

Four times in these three Chapters Jesus has used the non-limiting concept of *whatever you ask*— for *power* to do greater things than I have done; or for *productivity* to bear much fruit; and even for *protection* and *provision* in the face of trials and death threats—ask and these shall be yours without limit.

As you ponder these things, dear Christian, let these truths transform you. If you have embraced Jesus Christ as your personal savior, the Spirit of God has conceived in you a child of sovereign God. This inward being, fathered by God, is in the *image* of God. God's ultimate intent voiced in the first week of creation has come to pass in you. Listen now as Peter explains what is happening in your being:

> *According as his divine power hath given unto us all things that pertain unto life and godliness, through the knowledge of him that hath called us to glory and virtue: Whereby are given unto us exceeding great and precious promises: that by these ye might be partakers of the divine nature . . . .*

Just think what this means! I have become a completely new spirit being—conceived by the sperm of God! When an earthly baby is conceived 23 chromosomes of the mother and 23 chromosomes of the father, containing all the genes of human characteristics, from two different families, blend into a new procreation.

A similar event has occurred in the spiritual. When I embraced Jesus Christ, a new spirit, comprised of both human and divine, was generated; as I develop in the womb of the old body through the metamorphosis of sanctification, a renewed soul *is developed, and through the miracle of resurrection, my new body will be birthed into eternity.*

This new person is a human/divine hybrid. I am a partaker of Divine nature. I am a participant in the genus of God.

I am a son of sovereign God!

Lesson Eight
INDWELLED BY GOD

*H*ear, O Israel: The LORD our God is one LORD: These words may be called the creed of the Jews. They form the *Shema*, in the Jewish morning and evening worship, which is the Hebrew word for Hear, meaning to hear with understanding. It is the single greatest instructional message from God to Israel in the Old Testament—*Our Jehovah is one Elohiym.*

This description of God is followed with the command that Jesus called the first and greatest commandment: *"And thou shalt love the LORD thy God with all thine heart, and with all thy soul, and with all thy might"* (Deuteronomy 6:4-5).

The concept of one God-Being is essential for the Biblical worldview and yet we have previously reviewed the three pictures presented in the first three chapters of Genesis. It is even more intriguing to note the grammar of the opening statement, *"In the beginning God created the heaven and the earth."* The word *God* is plural, and by a primary law of grammar a plural noun, as subject of a sentence, demands a plural verb; yet, the verb *created* is in the singular number. Here, is at least a hint of a plurality within a unitary being.

Of God the Father the Psalmist declared: *"Oh my God . . . .Of old hast thou laid the foundation of the earth: and the heavens are the work of thy hands"* (102:24-25). Of Jesus, the New Testament declares: *"For by him were all things created, that are in heaven, and that are in earth*

. . ." (Colossians 1:16). And of the Spirit the Bible asserts, *"By his Spirit he hath garnished the heavens* (Job 26:13) ,and *"Thou sendest forth thy Spirit, they are created; and Thou renewest the face of the earth"* (Psalm 104:30). Hence, Elohiym, while being One is yet three-in-one.

Think back to the statement of God's ultimate intent, *"Let us make man in our image . . . ."* and God created man *spirit, soul*, and *body* (1 Thessalonians 5:23). Our spirit is our God-consciousness; our soul is self-consciousness in a context of social awareness— the citadel of our emotions: and our body is matter with consciousness through sensory perception. Yet, I am one being—spirit, soul, and body—each of which operates somewhat separately in order to accomplish its unique function but is dependent upon unity for life's performance.

Based upon this concept of One God with three persons, clarified for our comprehension by our tri-part being, spirit, soul, and body— reflecting the image of God, let us listen carefully to the promises of Jesus as he prepared His disciples for His exit.

The Promise of the Son

As Jesus sought to calm the troubled minds of His disciples, He desired to assure them that they would not be left alone in this troubled world. He was leaving to prepare a place for their future reunion, but they would not be left without His presence and His power. He said, *"I will pray the Father, and he shall give you another comforter . . . ."* The word *comforter* is a translation of the Greek word *parakletos*—one called alongside, which means an advocate, an intercessor, and enabler. Jesus

> The word *comforter* is a translation of the Greek word *parakletos*—
> one called alongside, which means an advocate, an intercessor, and
> enabler.

had been to them a counsellor, a guide, a friend, while he was with them. He had instructed them, had borne with their prejudices and ignorance, and had administered consolation to them in the times of despondency. But he was about to leave them. The other Comforter was to be given as a compensation for His absence, or to perform the offices toward them which He would have done if He had remained personally with them. And from this we may learn, in part, what is the office work of the Spirit. It is to furnish to all Christians the instruction and consolation which would be given by the personal presence of Jesus.

The remainder of the promise was that He, the Spirit would remain with them. Throughout the Old Testament the Spirit of God had come upon men for a particular task and would then leave. We read of this constantly throughout the period of the judges of Israel. The people would sin and forget God and God would raise up a leader and the Spirit of the LORD came upon him . . . . This happened to Othnial, Gideon, Jephthah and others but would later depart. However, Jesus promised the Comforter that He might abide with you forever. The word *abide* means *to stay with you*, and the term *forever* means *for the duration*—for life.

The Spirit of God is then described in terms of the work He is to perform for the disciple, He is called *Spirit of truth.* His exact work, as described later in verse 26, is to teach and bring things to remembrance. He will take of Christ's truths and make it plain to them.

Jesus gave His disciples greater consolation as He declared (verses 17-20) you know this Comforter—*He has been with you, and shall be in you.* I will not leave you without a Comforter—I will come to you. And then He declares: *"At that day ye shall know that I am in my Father, and ye in me and I in you."*

We spoke of this in the last chapter and described it as being totally immersed in God. The God who is One-God indwells the believer. This is not just a chip of God, this is not just the force of God being with us—the sovereign creator of all creation takes up residence in His prime creation whom He has made through procreative processes in His own image and likeness.

The Promise of the Father

Jesus had now endured death for each member of Adam's race, but the Spirit of God had quickened Him with resurrection power. For forty days He had shewed Himself alive by many infallible proofs. He now assembled them for His exodus to heavenly exaltation. He had given them His Great Commission, His great Promise and now one last command was uttered: *"Tarry ye in the city of Jerusalem, until ye be endued with power from on high"* (Luke 24:49). He called this event for which they were to wait—*the promise of the Father!*

John the Baptist had described Jesus to the crowds that came to him for baptism, *"I indeed baptize you with water; but one mightier than I cometh, the latchet of whose shoes I am not worthy to unloose: he shall baptize you with the Holy Ghost and with fire"* (Luke 3:16).

Jesus had also described this *Promise of the Father"* by saying: *"Ye shall be baptized with the Holy Ghost not many days hence."*

Jesus' followers had obeyed their Lord and continued with one accord in prayer and supplication worshipping together until the Day of Pentecost. Suddenly, with the sound of a rushing mighty wind, tongues of fire rested upon each of them and they were all filled with the Holy Ghost . . . .

The Promise of Jesus and the Promise of the Father had come to pass as God took up residence in each Spirit conceived Christian.

The Promise of the Spirit

We usually refer to the Spirit of God as the Holy Spirit. This is not His name but it is His office title. It describes what He intends to do in us. First, we must recognize that He is the agent of our salvation. We studied in the lesson on the *Ladder to God* how the Spirit of God guides us into contact with God's promises in His Word. He then illuminates our minds, convicts us of our sin and draws us to accept Jesus Christ as our personal savior. As we embrace Jesus as our Savior, it is the Spirit of God that conceives within us a child of God and takes up this indwelling presence in us.

Promise of Sonship. It was John, writing by the inspiration of the Spirit of God, who declared (John 1:12), *"But as many as received him, to them gave he power to become sons of God, even to those that believe on his name."* As this spiritual conception takes place and the Spirit takes up residence in us He causes us to cry out, *"Abba Father"* and bears witness with our spirit that we are children of God (Romans 8:15-17). and if we are children, the Spirit reminds us that we are heirs of sovereign God—heirs, jointly with Jesus Christ.

Promise of Ownership. Paul directs attention in his letter to the Ephesian Christians that our entire purpose on earth is to exist for the praise of God's glory (1:12). Hence, the Spirit was promised by the Father as His Signet to declare His ownership and authentication of our family relationship. A signet was a ring or stamp that was used to leave an imprint on a document or deed that authenticated it.

Paul used this descriptive language twice in this Book and again in 2 Corinthians 1:22 "Who hath also sealed us, and given the earnest of the Spirit in our hearts." God has provided evidence that the Holy Spirit within us is His seal: *"In whom ye also trusted, after that ye heard the word of truth, the gospel of your salvation: in whom also after that ye believed, ye were sealed with that holy Spirit of promise* (Ephesians 1:13). Furthermore, this seal will endure until the day of our redemption when we enter into our inheritance (Ephesians 4:30).

Not only is the Spirit of God the signet seal of God, imprinted upon our lives for all both in heaven and in earth to see, but He is also the earnest payment *"Being confident of this very thing, that he which hath begun a good work in you will perform it until the day of Jesus Christ* (Philippians 1:6). The Holy Spirit, resident in our lives, is God's guarantee to us that what He has begun in us He will perform until the day of Christ.

Promise of Mentorship. We have previously listened as Jesus taught His disciples for the final time before His death in the upper room. As He promised them another Comforter, He described this one as "the *Spirit of truth*" (John 14:17). Jesus said (16:13-14), "*He will guide you into all truth . . .He shall take of mine and shew it unto you*"—make it plain to you. This is truly the work of a teacher or personal mentor.

We earlier studied the work of *illumination* done by the Spirit of Truth as He draws a person to God. We defined illumination as the work of the Spirit of God causing a person to comprehend God's Truth. This is exactly the function Jesus promised His disciples that the *Comforter* would perform in their lives and minds.

The Spirit's work of illumination is absolutely necessary because (2 Corinthians 4:4-6) "*the god of this world hath blinded the minds of them which believe not, lest the light of the glorious gospel of Christ, who is the image of God should shine unto them.*" However, Paul clarifies the difference between the unbeliever and the believer was God's illumination (verse 6), "*For God, who commanded the light to shine out of darkness, hath shined in our hearts, to give the light of the knowledge of the glory of God in the face of Jesus Christ.*"

This enlightenment, causing us to comprehend, is now the perpetual work of the indwelling Spirit of Truth as he mentors us in the knowledge of Truth. Paul prayed for the Ephesian Christians (Ephesians 1:17-19) "*That the God of our Lord Jesus Christ, the Father of glory, may give unto you the spirit of wisdom and revelation in the knowledge of him: The eyes of your understanding being enlightened; that ye may know what is the hope of his calling, and what the riches of the glory of his inheritance in the saints, And what is the exceeding greatness of his power to usward who believe, according to the working of his mighty power."*

We are commanded to *study to show ourselves approved unto God,* but we are not alone. As we study we have a personal tutor and mentor giving us that spirit of wisdom and revelation to truly comprehend the truth of the knowledge that God has revealed in his Word— truth that we can never discover by ourselves. The Spirit of Truth is taking of Christ's Word and making it plain to us.

Promise of Transformation. The promise that we can experience transformation is based on the mentoring work of the Spirit of Truth. After Paul in Romans 12:1 begs Christians to present their bodies as living sacrifices, he then turns his attention to the mind: *"be not conformed to this world: but be ye transformed by the renewing of your mind . . . ."*

The word translated *transformed* is the Greek word *metamorphoo* from which we get the English word *metamorphose.* This means a complete change in physical structure or character. This describes the change from an ugly caterpillar to a beautiful butterfly. It is the concept that Paul uses in writing this God inspired Book. When applied to us it forcefully reminds us of God's *Ultimate Intent for man* as He said in Genesis 1:26. *"Let us make man in our image after our likeness."*

God has already achieved the first part of this intent through the procreation of our new *creature.* We are in the image of God as Spirit conceived sons and daughters of sovereign God. Now He has sent His Holy

Spirit (Spirit that maketh holy), into our inner man to transform us into His likeness—transformed into the Character of Jesus Christ. It is the realization of what God foreknew, and for which God predestinated us—"*to be conformed to the image of his Son* (Romans 8:29)."

Since this Transformation begins with the renewing of our mind we will study this in detail in the next lesson, and study how we are conformed to the *likeness* of His Son in a later lesson.

The Promise of Power. The work to which Jesus commissioned His disciples was characterized by these words (John 14:12-14) in the upper room discourse: "*He that believeth on me, the works that I do shall he do also; and greater works than these shall he do; because I go unto my Father, and whatsoever ye shall ask in my name, that will I do . . . If ye shall ask anything in my name, I will do it.*"

The power to perform these *greater works* was promised by Jesus. Immediately afterward Jesus voiced the promise of the Comforter. We have already discussed the meaning of the Greek word for Comforter which has an array of meanings. It is somewhat difficult, therefore, to fix the precise meaning of the word. It may be translated either advocate, monitor, teacher, or helper. As a helper it also conveys the concept of an enabler.

We studied Paul's prayer for the Ephesian saints as he prayed for their enlightenment (1:17-18). Note what follows that petition: "*And what is the exceeding greatness of his power to usward who believe, according to the working of his mighty power, Which he wrought in Christ, when he raised him from the dead, and set him at his own right hand in the heavenly places . . . .*"

The same God-Spirit, that we first encountered in the second verse in the Bible brooding over formless chaos to bring form from formlessness, was a God of unfathomable power. The Spirit that brought again Jesus from the dead was a God of immeasurable power. This is the same God that now resides in us as Christians to work in us and through us. He is the one who can break the power of sin in our lives and transform us into the *likeness* of God.

> This is the same God that now resides in us as Christians to work in us and through us. He is the one who can break the power of sin in our lives and transform us into the *likeness* of God.

Temple of God

A Temple was an edifice erected to a god with the understanding that it was devoted to his service and with the understanding that it was the special residence of that god. The Temple in Jerusalem was a magnificent building totally dedicated to God's service and where the radiance of the glory of God demonstrated the presence of YAHWEH.

Paul used these two concepts when he asked (1 Corinthians 6:19-20) the Christians in Corinth: "*What? know ye not that your body is the temple of the Holy Ghost which is in you, which ye have of God, and ye are not your own? For ye are bought with a price: therefore glorify God in your body . . . .*"

This may be the most elevated concept we have discovered in our study of the indwelling Spirit of God. We have been purchased by the blood of Jesus. We are dead to sin through the death of our Lord, our inner man has been conceived by God and with this new spirit we are to control the body and the soul. God, the Spirit, has taken up residence in us—we are the temple of God.

As this Temple, we are completely dedicated to the service of God, and we are the residence of God. No wonder Paul exclaimed, "You are not your own . . .therefore glorify God in your body." It is interesting to note that the words *"and in your spirit, which are Gods;"* did not appear in the original text and were added by translators. It is further interesting that the body as a physical material body is the Temple of God. It is the *outward* man that our *inward* man must learn to control. It is in and through the body that we are enjoined to Glorify God. The inward man is to be transformed by the renewing of our mind, but the outward man is to be controlled by the inward man as a Temple dedicated to God's service and reserved for God as His residence.

The inward man is to be transformed by the renewing of our mind, but the outward man is to be controlled by the inward man as a Temple dedicated to God's service and reserved for God as His residence. Therefore, Glorify God in your body!

Therefore, Glorify God in your body!

"For who hath known the mind of the Lord, that he may instruct him? But we have the mind of Christ!"

1 Corinthians 2:16

Lesson Nine
THE MIND OF CHRIST

T he mind of man is the seat of will, decision, and intellect. Several words in both the Old Testament and New Testament translated by the English word *mind* provide different emphases to this control mechanism of man. As God commanded Old Testament Israel to love Him, He said: *"And thou shalt love the LORD thy God with all thine heart, and with all thy soul, and with all thy might"* (Deuternomy 6:5).

The word translated *heart* in the above verse is often translated *mind,* and it is used for the feelings, the will, and the intellect; as well as to express the center of the being. The word *soul* literally means a *"living breathing creature"* but is also used to identify the self-desire motivation of man and is the psychological ego-desire control system to which God "gave man over" at the fall.

Jesus quoted this verse when asked about the greatest commandment: *"And thou shalt love the Lord thy God with all thy heart, and with all thy soul, and with all thy mind, and with all thy strength: this is the first commandment"* (Mark 12:30). In the Greek text a form of the word *nous* adds even a stronger concept of the *mind* to the Hebrew text than is conveyed by the English text. *Nous* is a very strong Greek word meaning the intellect, i.e. mind (divine or human; in thought, feeling, or will).

The Mind in Original Creation

In the original creation man was created in the *image* of God with the opportunity to become *after His*

In the original creation man was created in the *image* of God with the opportunity to become *after His likeness.* *likeness.* The mind was the control center where the intellect and the will could choose to obey God. This choice had both a negative and a positive option. Adam was told to eat of the fruit of all the trees except the Tree of Knowledge of Good and Evil. Clustered among the permitted fruit was the Tree of Life, and since God later drove man from the Garden, following his failure to obey, lest he eat of the Tree of Life and live forever in his sin, we know that choosing the Tree of Life previous to his disobedience would have completed Adam forever in the image and likeness of God.

However, when tempted, Eve's biological being saw the fruit and craved to eat and her psychological being desired to be wise, her mind gave in to her drives and desires and failed. Likewise, Adam although he was not deceived like his wife, could not refrain, after Eve had eaten, and surrendered to his drives and desires and sinned. Hence, in both of them the mind failed in both its intellectual function and its will function and allowed the flesh and the soul to usurp the mind's control.

In Chapter Two we studied (Romans 1) how God gave man over to the control of the psychological ego-desire system, the biological drive system, and the demonic mind. Spiritual death was the penalty for sin, the mind became the instrument of Satan, and the psychological and biological natures became the controlling agencies of human endeavors.

The Mind in the New Procreation

We have already studied the new creation attributed to the spirit conception of the Christian. We are a new creation, members of a new race. This new being is a procreation of God—a child of God. Hence, we know that our inward being is in the image of God, although it is an infant image that needs growth and development. Peter recognizes when he declares: *"Wherefore laying aside all malice, and all guile, and hypocrisies, and envies, and all evil speakings, As newborn babes, desire the sincere milk of the word, that ye may grow thereby* (1 Peter 2:1-2).

Furthermore, we know that this new being has to have a new, but undeveloped mind. Paul confirms this fact *"For who hath known the mind of the Lord, that he may instruct him? But we have the mind of Christ* (1 Corinthians 2:16). This reality is that we, who have been conceived of the Spirit of God, not only are a new being but this new being has a new mind. It is this reality that Paul again addresses in Ephesians 4:22-24: *"That ye put off concerning the former conversation the old man, which is corrupt according to the deceitful lusts; And be renewed in the spirit of your mind; And that ye put on the new man, which after God is created in righteousness and true holiness."*

It is very clear that it is, by the new mind operating in the new man, that is to control the old Adam man in whose body the new man resides. And furthermore, it is abundantly clear that this new mind needs to grow and develop. In Romans 12:1-2 we are commanded: *"I beseech you therefore, brethren, by the mercies of God, that ye present your bodies a living sacrifice, holy, acceptable unto God, which is your reasonable service. And be not conformed to this world: but be ye transformed by the renewing of your mind, that ye may prove what is that good, and acceptable, and perfect, will of God."*

The word transformed is the Greek word *metamorphoo* from which we get our English word *metamorphose* which means a complete change in appearance and character. In an earlier study we explained this transformation as when the ugly worm is transformed by metamorphoses into the beautiful butterfly. This signified the complete change in actions and character of the old man as the new man takes charge through the control of the new mind. This transformation is triggered by the *"renewing of the mind."*

This renewing of the mind is a growth and development process that is more than simply filling it with new data and knowledge. It is a process of restructuring the mental processing. Even though we have the mind of Christ—a new spiritual mind, it still works in concert with the physical brain and the *human psyche.* The brain, like the hard drive in our computer is filled with data from past experiences and it interprets that data from the values, and worldview of the old nature.

Hence, the Biblical commands given through the writings of Paul we quoted above demands that our minds be renovated which in turn drives our spiritual transformation in life and character.

This renewing of the mind is a process of restructuring the mental processing.

Restructuring the Mind in Desire and Attitude

We learned in Lesson Two that when man chooses his own desire rather than God's Ultimate Intent that God turned him over to an ego-desire system. This self-centeredness became the ruling passion of Adam's race. Thus the first step in reversing this motivational passion must be directed to redirecting our ego-desire. In the upper room just after Judas had gone out to betray Jesus, Jesus said to the remaining disciples: "*A new commandment I give unto you, That ye love one another; as I have loved you, that ye also love one another*" (John 13:34). Love is a complete opposite of ego-desire, it is desire to give to another for another's good. It is the essence of the first two great commands as identified by Jesus in the first page of this lesson:

And thou shalt love the Lord thy God with all thy heart, and with all thy soul, and with all thy mind, and with all thy strength: This is the first commandment. And the second is like, namely this, Thou shalt love thy neighbour as thyself (Mark 12:30-31).

This redirecting of the ruling passion of life from self and ego-desire to God and other people is the very first target in our renovation of the mind. This renovation must be done by the Spirit of God much like He transformed the precreation formless chaos and ordered creation which God pronounced good. We read of the fruit of the Spirit in Galatians 5:22-24: "*But the fruit of the Spirit is love, joy, peace, longsuffering, gentleness, goodness, faith, meekness, temperance: against such there is no law. And they that are Christ's have crucified the flesh with the affections and lusts.*"

This fruit, born of the Spirit of God, has to do with the desires and attitudes of the psychological nature of man which controls his actions toward God, people, self and circumstances of life. This is the most radical renovation of the mind and results in the transformation of life and character into the "likeness" of God. We will study this again in a later lesson.

Paul summarized this transformation in his command to the Philippian Christians: *Let this mind be in you, which was also in Christ Jesus: Who, being in the form of God, thought it not robbery to be equal with God: But made himself of no reputation, and took upon him the form of a servant, and was made in the likeness of men: And being found in fashion as a man, he humbled himself, and became obedient unto death, even the death of the cross. Wherefore God also hath highly exalted him, and given him a name which is above every name: That at the name of Jesus every knee should bow, of things in heaven, and things in earth, and things under the earth; And that every tongue should confess that Jesus Christ is Lord, to the glory of God the Father* (Philippians 2:5-11).

The mind of Christ, although He was in the form or image of God, did not make His decisions based on His self image or desire, but His love for lost humans drove His decision to become man. Then as a man He humbled himself and became the sacrificial lamb of God to take away the sin of the world. These attitudes and actions form the pattern of mind that we are to emulate in the renovation of our mind.

Paul then completed the above command with the following summation: *'Therefore, my beloved, as ye have always obeyed . . . . work out your own salvation with fear and trembling. For it is God which worketh in you both to will and to do of his good pleasure" (Verses* 12-13). We are therefore admonished to work on this renewing of our minds knowing that God is working in us both to will, the deliberate choosing of the mind, and to do of His desire. Hence, the metamorphosis of the soul is the complete objective of our sanctification.

> Hence, the metamorphosis of the soul is the complete objective of our sanctification.

Restructuring the Mind from Carnal to Spiritual

The final control center of man is the biological components which are constantly demanding to satisfy drives and appetites. This is the physical body made from the dust of the earth which shall also return to dust. It is described in the Bible as the outward man, carnal or fleshly, the body of death, and an earthen vessel.

Paul, writing in Romans 8, described the control center of the flesh which he identified as the carnal mind:

> *For they that are after the flesh do mind the things of the flesh; but they that are after the Spirit the things of the Spirit. For to be carnally minded is death; but to be spiritually minded is life and peace. Because the carnal mind is enmity against God: for it is not subject to the law of God, neither indeed can be. So then they that are in the flesh cannot please God* (Verses 4-8).

The carnal mind seeks to satisfy the body's drives and appetites and is an enemy to the mind of the spirit that can control the body so that its deeds may please God. The great contrast in this passage is when the carnal mind controls, we walk after the flesh, and when the spiritual mind controls, we walk after the spirit. Moreover, the scripture continues, *But ye are not in the flesh, but in the Spirit, if so be that the Spirit of God dwell in you . . . . And if Christ be in you, the body is dead because of sin; but the Spirit is life because of righteousness. But if the Spirit of him that raised up Jesus from the dead dwell in you, he that raised up Christ from the dead shall also quicken your mortal bodies by his Spirit that dwelleth in you* (Romans 8:9-11).

Here again is repeated the truth presented in Romans 3 that we died in Christ's death and the body is dead, but we are a new spirit being indwelled by God and empowered by the Spirit of resurrection to control the actions of the body.

> **The Christian is a new spirit being indwelled by God and empowered by the Spirit of resurrection to control the actions of the body.**

Going back a chapter to Romans 7 we read of the struggle that Paul describes that went on in his own mind and body. He understood the flesh and the carnal nature and declared in verse 8 that there was nothing good in his flesh. He went on to say that he had the capacity to choose or to will, but that he ran into a problem how to perform what he knew was good. He described this inner conflict in verse 19: *"For the good that I would I do not: but the evil which I would not, that I do."*

He understood why the conflict raged and he concluded (verse 20) *"Now if I do that I would not, it is no* more I that do it, but sin that dwelleth in me." Here he identified what he described in 2 Corinthians as the *inward* man of the spirit and the *outward* man of the flesh. We still reside in the womb of the old man who is dead and dying, although we, the new creatures, have been conceived by God and have the authority and power to refuse the control of the drives and appetites of the flesh.

Paul then summarized a fantastic truth that every one of us must comprehend in order to live after the control of the spirit. He declared (verse 21-22), " *I find then a law*, (or a principle) *that, when I would do good, evil is present with me. For I delight in the law of God after the inward man."*

This is a reality that most of us have discovered. Just when we want desperately to please God, evil presents itself in relentless fashion. And we must conclude as Paul did, there is a law in my fleshly members that constantly wars against the law of my mind. I have the mind of Christ that delights to do God's will, but I have the body of fallen Adam, a body of clay that demands to have its drives and appetites satisfied. It is an unending warfare and struggle of two control centers of the mind— the mind of the flesh and the mind of the spirit.

As Paul reflected on the struggle he cried (verse 24) *"O wretched man that I am! who shall deliver me from the body of this death?"* But then he contemplated the new man and the new mind and shouted with praise (verse 25) *"I thank God through Jesus Christ our Lord. So then with the mind I myself serve the law of God; but with the flesh the law of sin."* He affirms that he has been delivered by the new mind of the new spirit being. When he, by this mind, refuses the demands of flesh he lives unto God. It is only, when he does not refuse these demands of the carnal, that he sins.

In the next verses (8:1-2) he shouts the victory *"There is therefore now no condemnation to them which are in Christ Jesus . . . For the law of the Spirit of life in Christ Jesus hath made me free from the law of sin and death."* In other words there is no adverse sentence against the sons and daughters of God living in a body of clay. The principle of active spirit control through the mind of Christ completely overcomes the law of sin in our members.

This can be illustrated as an airplane sits on the runway. It is grounded by gravity, but if it speeds down the runway and the air racing over the airfoils generates aerodynamic lift—this law of aerodynamics overcomes the law of gravity. As we walk by means of the Spirit we overcome the law of flesh.

Restructuring the Mental Processing of the Mind

We have seen several times in our study of spiritual formation that transformation of life flows from the renovation of our mind. *". . . be ye transformed by the renewing of your mind* (Romans 12:2).

This restructuring of the mind is comparable to the installation of a new operating system and the reformatting of a hard drive in our computer. In Jesus' very first sermon which we refer to as the Sermon on the Mount, He addresses this vital restructuring of the mind. Jesus began His ministry with a command: *"From that time Jesus began to preach, and to say, Repent: for the kingdom of heaven is at hand."*

The word *repent* means *"change your mind."* It is not only a command to change the perceptions of your mind, it is a command to restructure your mind. This entire sermon is a cry to change from man's perceptions to God's truth, as demonstrated in the beatitudes early in chapter 5, and the challenge to change their mind about sin later in the chapter. When He gets to verse 19 in Chapter 6 He begins to summarize His message: *Lay not up for yourselves treasures upon earth, where moth and rust doth corrupt, and where thieves break through and steal: But lay up for yourselves treasures in heaven, where neither moth nor rust doth corrupt, and where thieves do not break through nor steal: For where your treasure is, there will your heart be also.*

Value System. A treasure is something that we value and Jesus is saying, "Change your mind about Values." It is on the basis of values that we make decisions and Jesus wants to probe our minds to determine whether we are making decisions on the basis of earthly values or heavenly values. In verses 25-33 He challenges us to think about the values that drive our decisions. *"Therefore I say unto you, Take no thought for your life, what ye shall eat, or what ye shall drink; nor yet for your body, what ye shall put on. Is not the life more than meat, and the body than raiment?"* The phrase "take no thought" literally means don't make decisions based on what you will eat, drink or clothing for your body.

> **The phrase *"take no thought"* literally means don't make decisions based on what you will eat, drink or clothing for your body..**

In verses 26 and 28 he points to the birds that the Father feedeth, and the flowers that grow without toiling. His point is that God takes care of these— aren't we of greater value than they? In verse 32 He points to the pagan world and states that these values of food, drink, and clothing are the values that drive the decisional focus of pagans. His final conclusion is embodied in the command: *"But seek ye first the kingdom of God, and his righteousness; and all these things* (what you will eat, drink, wear) *shall be added unto you."*

The mind of the spirit must be restructured with a Biblical Value System. This is the processing system for all decisions.

Interpretive System. The second part of the mental processing system has to do with learning and knowledge. This is known as a worldview and provides the interpretation of all knowledge and learning.

Jesus addressed this reprogramming of the mind through an interesting illustration in verses 22-23: *The light of the body is the eye: if therefore thine eye be single, thy whole body shall be full of light. But if thine eye be evil, thy whole body shall be full of darkness. If therefore the light that is in thee be darkness, how great is that darkness!*

He speaks of a disease of the eye in which one eye focuses a few inches and the other eye focuses a few feet. Here the word single is used to address a single focus, which provides clarity and light. He describes the eye as the source of light in the body, and applies it to the vehicle to give light to the spirit. Paul spoke of this to the Ephesian Christians when he said: *"The eyes of your understanding being enlightened; that ye may know what is the hope of his calling, and what the riches of the glory of his inheritance in the saints".*

There are several distinct worldviews by which men interpret knowledge. These worldviews are comprised of four concepts: God or god, man (and other created beings), matter, and time. Basically there is a scientific-materialism worldview, a humanistic worldview, and a Biblical worldview. These form the bases for interpreting knowledge.

We must make certain that our eyes are of a single Biblical focus and that we interpret all reality from a Biblical Worldview.

Authority System. The third system of the mental processing system is an authority system. Jesus spoke of this in verse 24: *"No man can serve two masters: for either he will hate the one, and love the other; or else he will hold to the one, and despise the other. Ye cannot serve God and mammon."*

Mammon is a Syriac word, a name given to an idol worshipped as the god of riches. The Jewish culture used the word to denote wealth. The meaning is, ye cannot serve the true God, and at the same time be supremely engaged and driven in obtaining the riches of this world.

THREE SYSTEMS OF THE MIND THAT MUST BE REPROGRAMED
1. Value System—basis for all decisions
2. Interpretive System—basis for learning
3. Authority System—regulates all behavior

Jesus is addressing a mental processing system that regulates all behavior. The basic issue is that no man can serve two masters. His drives and energy will be driven to pursue that which provides authority and purpose to his life. That which he loves, he desires, and it becomes the magnet that draws his life.

The Mind is the control center of man. Unredeemed persons are controlled by the reprobate or as we have called it a demonic mind. This is why in the pre-flood world every imagination of man was only evil continually. When a person becomes a Christian and is a spirit conceived child of God, he receives a new mind, which is like a new operating system in your computer. The Bible uses the term, the mind of Christ. Now this new operating system must program the hard drive of your memory, will, and intellect. Listen again to Paul's direction: *"And be not conformed to this world: but be ye transformed by the renewing of your mind, that ye may prove what is that good, and acceptable, and perfect, will of God"* (Romans 12:2).

This renewing comes from the application of the Word of God to restructure the systems by which you make decisions, interpret knowledge, and respond to authority; and you must file the truth of God's revelation in the data banks of your memory. This changed mind is that which will control the total conduct of your life that you might be conformed to the *likeness* of Jesus Christ.

> *Thou wilt keep him in perfect peace, whose mind is stayed on thee: because he trusteth in thee* (Isaiah 26:3).

Lesson Ten
LIVING THE CHRIST LIFE

The restructuring of our minds, resulting in the control of our psychological and biological natures by the mind of Christ within us, now provides the reality of transforming the character of our lives to the likeness of Jesus Christ. This is the ultimate desire of God which we have traced from Genesis 1:26 to the present moment.

The struggle of the outward man against the inward man, which is the mind of the spirit controlling the law of sin that is in our members, is that operation which the Holy Spirit empowers to conform us to the likeness of Christ. It is the constant operation Paul described in 2 Corinthians 10:4-5: *For the weapons of our warfare are not carnal, but mighty through God to the pulling down of strong holds;) Casting down imaginations, and every high thing that exalteth itself against the knowledge of God, and bringing into captivity every thought to the obedience of Christ.*

Our attention is directed, in the above verse, to the *weapons of our warfare.* First, the battle arena is within our mind, and our weapons are the mind of Christ which has been restructured as the mind of the spirit by the renovation (renewing) of the mind as discussed in the last lesson.

With these weapons we are enabled to *"pull down strongholds."* This is the "change of the mind" (repent) that Jesus addressed in His great sermon on the mount, as we change from man's conclusions to God's truth.

This is the process of mental restructuring we discussed in the previous lesson which resulted in a Biblical Value System as the basis for all decisions; the structuring of a Biblical Interpretative System (worldview) by which we interpret all learning and knowledge; and the restructuring of a Biblical Authority System from which all behavior ensues.

The next great theater of battle deals with "*casting down imaginations, and every high thing that exalteth itself against the knowledge of God (2 Cor. 10:5).*" The word *imaginations* literally means *reasonings* and conclusions of man that opposes the *knowledge of God*. The objectives of this raging battle is to bring every thought into submission to Christ. The word translated *thought* literally means every *perception*. A perception is how our brain interprets reality. Every thought—every conclusion of our brain must be in submission to Christ, or in agreement to Biblical truth.

These verses have given us a description of what really happens within the function of our mind which produces the transformed life we have discussed in the last two lessons.

Transformed Behavior

We will now turn our attention to *transformed* behavior that is produced by the functioning of the *renewed* mind energized by the power of God in us.

In Romans 5 after we were introduced to the reality of our justification and the peace with God which it brought to us, there is an outstanding reality pronounced for us: "*For if, when we were enemies, we were reconciled to God by the death of his Son, much more, being reconciled, we shall be saved by his life."* We recognize the vast importance of the death of Christ for our salvation, but now the language of Paul suggests that there is something more important than His death. He uses the term, *"Much more"* to point us to something of even greater value. Can anything be more important than the death of Christ?

As a non-Christian there is nothing more important than the death of Jesus; but now for the Christian who has accepted Jesus Christ as his personal savior and has been saved by His death, there is an even greater reality—*we shall be saved by His life.*

OUR TWO GREAT SALVATIONS
Salvation from Penalty of Sin—*by the Death of Christ!*
Salvation from the Power of Sin—*by the Life of Christ!*

Power for Transformed Behavior. When we accepted Christ and entered into His death we were saved from the penalty of sin and entered into everlasting life. *"For God so loved the world, that he gave his only begotten Son, that whosoever believeth in him should not perish, but have everlasting life"* (John 3:16). Now we are promised salvation from the power of sin—*saved by His life.*

In Galatians 2:20 both salvation from the penalty of sin and salvation from the power of sin are depicted:

I am crucified with Christ: nevertheless I live; yet not I, but Christ liveth in me: and the life which I now live in the flesh I live by the faith of the Son of God, who loved me, and gave himself for me.

Although I was crucified with Christ as He died my death, I was also raised in His resurrection. Therefore, I now live—*Christ liveth in me.* The life I now live in the flesh, I live by the faith of the Son of God. This is being saved by His life—saved from the power sin seeks to employ through my psychological and biological components of this earthly life.

I know this sounds a little strange and perhaps even mysterious. In fact even Paul wrote that this reality is a mystery. *Even the mystery which hath been hid from ages and from generations, but now is made manifest to his saints: To whom God would make known what is the riches of the glory of this mystery among the Gentiles; which is Christ in you, the hope of glory* (Colossians 1:26-29).

He who died for us was to live in us, and fill our whole souls with His own purity. No indwelling sin can be tolerated by an indwelling Christ; for he came into the world to save His people from their sins.

The Process of Transformed Behavior. The question that often arises in the mind of the Christian who knows that he has been saved from the power of sin, is "How can I do that?" We understand what God desires, but we, knowing the power of the flesh in which we reside, question, how it is possible? Paul enters into the answer to this in Romans 6. He has just declared that where sin abounded, God's grace had much more abounded. So he raised the question: "*Shall we continue in sin, that grace may abound?*" No, No— "*God forbid. How shall we, that are dead to sin, live any longer therein?*"

This is the question that must be comprehended by us in order that the transformation of life become a reality in our every day experience.. We must know what the Biblical phrases we have recently quoted mean— crucified with Christ, dead to sin, baptized into His death. This is the basic issue that God desires we learn from Romans 6. In verses 3, 6, and 9 there are three facts of spiritual dynamics that we must know. You see, behavior is driven by the comprehension of the mind— As a man thinketh in is heart, so is he.

The first truth (verse 3) is that illustrated by our baptism. *"Know ye not, that so many of us as were baptized into Jesus Christ were baptized into his death?"* Our union with Christ is a death union. Death was the payment for sin, and Jesus took our sin upon Him and submitted to death for you and me—and for each of the family members of Adam. What does death really mean?

Jesus by the death of the cross became insensible to all surrounding objects, as the dead always are. He ceased to see, and hear, and was as though they were not. He was laid in the cold grave, and they did not affect or influence him. So Paul says that he became insensible to the Law as a means of justification; to the world; to ambition and the love of money; to the pride and pomp of life, and to the dominion of evil and hateful passions. They lost their power over him; they ceased to influence and control him.

To be dead with Christ, to be crucified with Him does not mean that we actual suffered the pangs of Jesus' death, but it does mean that we have been released from the power that the old nature once exerted over us.

The second great truth we must comprehend is in verses 6 and 7: *"Knowing this, that our old man is crucified with him, that the body of sin might be destroyed, that henceforth we should not serve sin. For he that is dead is freed from sin."* Once again we demonstrate that the entire truth is all about control and our control systems. The controls of the old nature were the psychological ego-desire system and the biological drive system. Our union with Christ in His death releases us from these powerful controls.

The exact words of these verses are very interesting. The meaning of the phrase "body of sin" has been argued by the scholars. Some believe it is just another way of identifying the "old man." Others find in it the intricate concept of sin having many different forces and vices, and still others argue that it demonstrates how sin has dominated our entire earthly nature as Paul describes it in his sad lament (7:24) *"O wretched man that I am! Who shall deliver me from the body of this death?"* One thing is certain, Christ's death destroyed this body of sin's control over us that we do not have to serve sin. We are freed from the control and dominance of Sin.

ONE THING IS CERTAIN
Christ's death destroyed this body of sin's control over us that we do not have to serve sin. We are freed from the control and dominance of Sin.

There is one more truth that we must comprehend: *"Knowing that Christ being raised from the dead dieth no more; death hath no more dominion over him. For in that he died, he died unto sin once: but in that he liveth, he liveth unto God"* (Romans 6:9-10). From these three statements of truth that we must comprehend there are three specific behaviors for us to achieve.

1. We should walk in newness of life (verse 4).
2. Wc should not serve sin (verse 6).
3. We should live unto God (verse 10).

The Product of Transformed Behavior. There are also three commands to those for whom Christ died and who had placed their faith in His death and His life. Our faith in His death frees us from the penalty of sin, and our faith in His life provides the power to refuse sin's control. Christ arose and death has no dominion over Him. He lives only to advance the glory of God. Based on this behavior of Jesus Christ, Paul now commands the Christian to (verse 11) *"Likewise reckon ye also yourselves to be dead indeed unto sin, but alive unto God through Jesus Christ our Lord."* The word *reckon* comes from accounting language, and means account it so, or post it. We are dead to sin—sin has no hold on us—but we live, let us like our resurrected Lord, live only to advance the glory of God. Transformed behavior chooses every thought, every deed, every behavior to glorify his Father.

The second command (verse 12) based on these truths is that we will refuse to be controlled by sin. Every time a temptation flashes across our mind, whether it be from the eye-gate, a carnal drive or an ego-lust the renewed mind refuses—"no, no you don't control me, I live only for my Father."

The third command follows from these first two: *"Neither yield ye your members as instruments of*

unrighteousness unto sin: but yield yourselves unto God,
as those that are alive from the dead, and your members
as instruments of righteousness unto God" (verse 12). Sin
can only become a behavior in our lives when we give it
permission to use a bodily member. We can allow our
minds to pursue it in our imaginations, or permit our
tongue, hand,
foot, or other
bodily member
perform an act.
But when we do
we are submitting

> **REMEMBER THIS!**
> Sin can only become a behavior in our lives
> when we give it permission to use a bodily
> member.

our members to be instruments of sin. This Bible
command is to refuse to present our members as sin's
instruments, but to submit these members unto God as
instruments of righteousness.

Obeying these three commands consummates
transformed behavior, demonstrates that sin has no
dominion over us, and proves that we are saved by
Christ's life. We are transformed into holy people as Peter
instructed us: *Wherefore gird up the loins of your mind,*
> *be sober, and hope to the end for the grace that is to*
> *be brought unto you at the revelation of Jesus Christ;*
> *As obedient children, not fashioning yourselves*
> *according to the former lusts in your ignorance: But*
> *as he which hath called you is holy, so be ye holy in*
> *all manner of conversation; Because it is written, Be*
> *ye holy; for I am holy* (1 Peter 1:13-16).

This reality of a transformed life fulfills God's
ultimate intent for His sons and daughters that we be in
the *image* and *likeness* of God. Paul expressed the single
motivation for this transformed life: *"For to me to live*
is Christ, and to die is gain (Phil. 1:21)."

Lesson Eleven

CONFORMED TO CHRIST'S LIKENESS

In the last two lessons we discovered that we have the mind of Christ, and discussed how our life can be transformed by the renewing of our mind. With the Spirit-directed mind of the *inward man* now in control of the old *outward man* the character of our lives can be transformed. Paul expressed this reality to the Church in Ephesus (4:14-15) when he directed that they be no more children, tossed to and fro by diverse doctrines and by crafty deceitful persons, *"But speaking the truth in love, may grow up into him in all things, which is the head, even Christ."* Growing up into Christ is not only giving Christ absolute authority over our life, but it is developing the very character of Jesus in our life.

Paul expressed this same possibility as he wrote to the Galatians (4:19): *"My little children, of whom I travail in birth again until Christ be formed in you."*

> Growing up into Christ is not only giving Christ absolute authority over our life, but it is developing the very character of Jesus in our life.

It is the role of the Holy Spirit—or Spirit that maketh holy, to shape the character of Jesus Christ in your life. This is an essential part of the process of renewing the *inward man* day-by-day. To know the character of a person, we analyze the traits which identify distinguishing features of one's personal nature. What are the distinguishing features of the personal nature of Jesus? These are the same ones that God wants positioned in our lives to demonstrate the likeness of Jesus Christ in us.

We have already studied that the Spirit of Truth has been stationed in our lives to glorify Christ. This glorification is demonstrated when the character traits of Jesus are evidenced within us. Paul speaks of this (Galatians 5:22-23) as the fruit of the Spirit. In this context he had described the works of flesh in terms of the sinful deeds that naturally flowed from Adam's fallen children, and then he contrasted them with ". . . *love, joy, peace, longsuffering, gentleness, goodness, faith, meekness, temperance . . .*" As fruit of the Spirit, it is strongly implied that this is the result of the Holy Spirit laboring within us—renewing our *inward man* day-by-day.

This fruit that can be produced within our lives consists of the character traits demonstrated in the life of Jesus Christ. When these traits become a normal pattern of our actions and reactions then Christ can be seen in us. Hence, as we continue our strategy for the ongoing renewal of our *inward person* these character traits form a curriculum for growth and development.

> When these traits become a normal pattern of our actions and reactions then Christ can be seen in us.

Although we are emphasizing the growth and development of the *inward* or *spirit-person,* we also know that this new creation still lives in the old body of flesh. Just as we discussed in the previous lessons, God has made it possible for the redeemed spirit-mind to take control of the yet unredeemed body and to put to death the deeds, or works, of the flesh. Therefore, as the fruit of the Spirit is borne in the *inward man,* the character traits of Jesus can be demonstrated even through the overt words, deeds, and actions of the *outward man.* As these demonstrate outwardly that the character of Christ has been formed inwardly it can clearly be known as conformity to the likeness of Jesus the Christ.

Love—the Cornerstone of Character

The first character trait of Jesus Christ that the Holy Spirit desires to fully actualize in your life is truly the cornerstone of godly character. It is the only one of these named traits that is both an essential element of God's nature as well as a characteristic of His actions: *"God is love,"* and *"God so loved the world."* God is *love* (1 John 4:8) just as certain as He is *light* (1:5), and He is *spirit* (John 4:24). Christianity is the only religion that sets forth its Supreme Being as Love. Other religions were created by man (Romans 1:23) as he changed the glory of the incorruptible God into images like man, birds, beasts and creeping things; and, of

> **Christianity is the only religion that sets forth its Supreme Being as Love.**

course, projected an image from his fallen nature of avarice, despotism, and anger demanding appeasement.

Love is a concept naturally foreign to fallen man. Consider for a moment, what is the opposite of love? Self and selfishness are the opposite of love. Fallen man's basic life drive is to have his own way. *"All we like sheep have gone astray, we have turned every one to his own way . . ."* (Isaiah 53:6). As we saw in Lesson Two the summary of the fall of man from Romans 1, man became controlled by his psychological ego-desire that demanded his own way, biological drives and appetites that demanded to be satisfied, and a demonic mind that constructed a worldview without God.

What is Love—What Does It Mean?

There are two words in the original language of the New Testament that are both translated into the English as *love*. There is another Greek term, not translated *love* in the New Testament but has sometimes been translated *love* in other writings. It is the word *eros*, from which we get the word *erotic,* and is more akin to *lust.* It is the description of sexual attraction and depicts a drive or motivation of man that is self-grasping.

Phileo is one of the Greek words translated *love* in the New Testament and denotes *a strong ardent feeling and affection for another person.* It is an affection usually seeking reciprocal affection and hence it is a self-sharing love. We see this word in English words such as Philadelphia, or philanthropy. It is usually thought of as brotherly love or a caring love for others. This word is never used in the Bible to designate man's love for God.

The second New Testament word translated love is the Greek *agapao* and denotes *an earnest and anxious desire for and an active and beneficent interest in the well-being of the one loved.* This is the kind of love that is both feeling and action. It is love that acts for the good of another—this is *self-giving love.*

We have just described the overt action resulting from three internal feelings or desires. It is impossible for us to get inside the person or describe the component of nature that produces love. "Love can be known only from the action it prompts."[1] When the Bible says that *God is love*, we recognize it is part of His nature, and His actions of love toward mankind flow from this essential component of His nature.

Man can by human nature express *self-grasping emotion and feelings*; he can express *self-sharing affection*; but he cannot by natural human nature *express self-giving love*. This is the love which is born of God—the fruit of the Spirit. John, in his great epistle of love (1 John 4:12) stated: "*If we love one another, God dwelleth in us, and his love is perfected in us.*" He had previously said (verse 8) that a person that does not love, does not know God. He further asserts (verse 13) that since God's love is perfected by God's dwelling in us, that this is how we know that we dwell in Him and He has given us of His indwelling Spirit. In verse 16-17 he summarizes this thought: "*God is love; and he that dwelleth in love dwelleth in God, and God in him. Herein is our love made perfect . . . .*"

Stop and ponder for a moment what the Bible is really telling us about ourselves. What level is our love? Are the words and deeds of my life *self-grasping, self-sharing*, or *selfless giving* for the momentary as well as the eternal welfare of another? Where am I in the growth and development of God's kind of love in my inward person? How fruitful has the Spirit of God been within my life in producing God's kind of love in me?

---

[1] *Vine's Expository Dictionary of Biblical Words*, Copyright (c)1985, Thomas Nelson Publishers

Growing in Christlike Love

No matter our age, every new beginning in the continued growth and development of the *inward person* must begin with a renewal of God's love within us. Look around at the people your life touches. What benefit are you being to each of them? Since love reaches out to esteem and benefit another, what benefit can you be to them? Since love is the opposite of selfishness what changes need to take place in your attitudes and actions to another person to demonstrate that you are dwelling in God and God is dwelling in you?

> **Since love is the opposite of selfishness what changes need to take place in your attitudes and actions to another person to demonstrate that you are dwelling in God and God is dwelling in you?**

There is a tendency even in Christians, to get a little more focused on self as we age. All of the demands and limitations of our *outward being* tend to make us a little more self oriented. This is why the *inward man* must take charge and depend upon the Spirit of God to produce the fruit of love in our life. There must be a willing mind to be Christlike in love, and a willing mind to refuse my self-desire. It is then that the harvest of love fruit increases—The character of Christ is being formed and fashioned in me. My Father will then look down and seeing my growing love exclaim, "You remind me of my first born son."

Finding Complete Fulfillment

Once again let's gaze within at the miracle God is fashioning in our spirit-person. As our outer physical being is drying up like an old squash, our inner spirit-conceived child of God is growing and developing with new vigor and vitality daily. Since God desires that this new creation become more and more like Jesus Christ, His Spirit within us is laboring to bear fruit—the fashioning of the character traits of God within us.

To have this fruit of the Spirit borne within our lives it takes the joint effort of the Holy Spirit and our renewed mind choosing correct action and refusing to give in to the desires and drives of the old nature. These choices must be made moment by moment—experience by experience. It is a great benefit to look ahead and prepare our mind for coming choices. As we rise each day it helps to pray, "Father, today I want to love like Jesus, I want to know joy, like Jesus. Help me to develop these character traits of Your life."

In the last section we focused on growing in love. Now we want to turn our attention to the next character trait named as "fruit of the Spirit—Joy!"

As Peter began to write his first epistle (1:1-9) to Christians who had been scattered by persecution he describes what God is doing in their lives which provides the growth and development of the spiritual life still entwined in the physical life—but resulting in *"joy unspeakable and full of glory."*

What is This Thing Called "Joy"?

The Old Testament saints spoke of joy, but it was always in relation to God's special provision for them. After his terrible sin, David prayed (Psalm 51:8-12) that God would create a clean heart within him and renew a right spirit. He begged not to be cast from God's presence but that God would make him hear joy and gladness, and then cried: *"Restore unto me the joy of my salvation . . . ."*

When the children of Israel held special feast days of worship, especially after they had been in rebellion, the description was often used, *"there was great joy in Jerusalem."* On one such occasion after the walls of Jerusalem had been rebuilt under the leadership of Nehemiah, the people gathered to listen to the reading of the law (8:1-10). Ezra had read from the Law from morning to midday, he had explained it and they understood. The people began to weep, but Nehemiah sent them away to eat and to drink and to rejoice for he declared: *"the joy of the Lord is your strength."*

The Psalmist (Psalm 27) testified that the Lord was his light, salvation and strength of life. He then spoke of his enemies encamped around him but declared that he would be confident because he had desired to dwell in the house of the Lord all the days of his life. He trusted God to hide him in His tabernacle and set him upon a rock. Because of this hope he would offer the *sacrifices of joy* and sing praises unto the Lord.

Isaiah (12:1-3) looked forward to redeemed Israel in the last days. Israel will rejoice because God has turned away His anger from them. They expressed their worship by declaring *"Therefore with joy shall we draw water out of the wells of salvation."*

All of these outbursts of joy by the people of the Old Testament suggest that they were expressing their complete satisfaction in Jehovah and what He had done for them.

Think back for a moment of the lives of the natural children of Adam controlled by their sinful being. Man's ego-desires drove him to have his own way—to seek his own fulfillment. His fleshly appetites and drives cried out to be satisfied. Man's momentary happiness resulted from his self-desire being fulfilled and his fleshly appetites and drives satisfied. We speak of these things as being pleasing to the ego and the flesh. The natural man's life is a constant cycle of seeking greater and greater desire-fulfillment, and greater and greater soul-satisfaction. But each is temporary and fleeting.

Take these ideas of pleasure understood by natural man and now move them to a higher plain of spiritual experience. Joy is similar to pleasure and happiness— but its cause is God. The driving motivation of natural man is to have his own way—this is his self-fulfillment. The motivation of our spiritual being is to do the will of God, our Father—to bring glory to Him. When we find our fulfillment in doing God's will—joy floods our being.

> WHEN WE FIND OUR FULFILLMENT IN DOING GOD'S WILL—
> JOY FLOODS OUR BEING.

The fleshly man is satisfied by such things as food and sex—these bring momentary satisfaction and pleasure. The spiritual man hungers and thirsts after righteousness—this satisfaction is joy and rejoicing.

The Curriculum of Joy

Learning to walk in joy is one of the most essential courses in the school of maturation. Although the Spirit of Truth longs to teach us, and longs to see this character trait of a holy life billowing up within us, we must desire above everything else to find our fulfillment in doing God's will.

In His final training session with His disciples before His death, Jesus told them He was going away to prepare a place for them, but that He would return for them. He told of the work that they were to do to glorify God, and promised them the indwelling presence of God. He described that they were to bear fruit and unveiled the vast potential of prayer. Then (John 15:11) He summarized, *"These things have I spoken unto you, that my joy might remain in you, and **that your joy might be full.**"* They were to discover that their complete satisfaction would be in God.

Jesus continued this discourse and told (16:1-4) them that they would be persecuted and even killed for His sake. He told them more of what the Spirit of Truth would achieve in their lives and reminded them again (16:23-24) that even in this dark day they could pray:

> *Whatsoever ye shall ask the Father in my name, he will give it you. Hitherto have ye asked nothing in my name: ask, and ye shall receive, that **your joy may be full**.*

Notice again, just like in the Old Testament, *joy* seems to be in contrast to, and even enhanced by adversity. James also agreed with this (James 1:2-3) when he declared: *My brethren, count it all joy when ye fall into divers temptations. Knowing this that the trying of your faith worketh patience.*

We began this chapter with reference to 1 Peter 1:3-9: *Blessed be the God and Father of our Lord Jesus Christ, which according to his abundant mercy hath begotten us again unto a lively hope by the resurrection of Jesus Christ from the dead, (4) To an inheritance incorruptible, and undefiled, and that fadeth not away, reserved in heaven for you, (5) Who are kept by the power of God through faith unto salvation ready to be revealed in the last time. (6) Wherein ye greatly rejoice, though now for a season, if need be, ye are in heaviness through manifold temptations: (7) That the trial of your faith, being much more precious than of gold that perisheth, though it be tried with fire, might be found unto praise and honour and glory at the appearing of Jesus Christ: (8) Whom having not seen, ye love; in whom, though now ye see him not, yet believing, ye rejoice with joy unspeakable and full of glory: (9) Receiving the end of your faith, even the salvation of your souls.*

In verses 3-5 Peter reminds us that we have been begotten by God unto a living hope which is an incorruptible inheritance reserved in heaven for us, and that we are being kept by the power of God through faith until we are revealed in the last time. However (verse 6), we are going through trials of persecution and hardships to refine our faith like gold is refined in a furnace of fire and it is for the same purpose. God desires our faith be refined so it will have praise when Jesus Christ appears. This is the same Jesus we now see only by faith, but Whom we shall see in glory—in Whom we rejoice with joy unspeakable and full of glory when we receive the completion of our salvation.

It is our unfailing hope in God that He will provide all that He has prepared for us, and the unflagging faith that constantly presses us toward the prize that floods our spirit with unspeakable joy. As God's glory becomes our fulfillment, and God's presence becomes our satisfaction—unspeakable joy will be our daily portion.

> As God's glory becomes our fulfillment, and God's presence becomes our satisfaction—unspeakable joy will be our daily portion.

The Shalom of God

In the final countdown hours awaiting death, Jesus calmed His disciples who were expressing fear and frustration. He had addressed their fears head on and admonished them, *"Let not your heart be troubled . . . ."* He had given them a flash forward of what He would be doing, and what they would be doing. He announced the coming of the "Comforter," the Holy Spirit sent from the Father to indwell the believer. Like oil poured on raging water He then promised His followers (John 14:27): *"Peace I leave with you, my peace I give unto you: not as the world giveth, give I unto you. Let not your heart be troubled, neither let it be afraid. "*

Peace is a character trait of Jesus Christ God desires to produce within our *inward* man by the cultivation of the Spirit of Holiness. He wants us to desire peace, experience peace, and practice peace. He wants us to display an aura of quietness, rest, and calm even in turbulent times and distressing conditions. *"Let not your heart be troubled"* is not only a cure for a definitive moment, but a character trait for the continuum of living.

> *Let not your heart be troubled*" is not only a cure for a definitive moment, but a character trait for the continuum of living.

Although God wants his youngest child to walk in peace, it is also a special need of aging folk to *"seek peace and pursue it"* (Psalms 34:14) as the extra burden of fears and troubles descend in the outer border of life. In the growth and development of the *inward man, peace* is a major attribute that must be given full attention as fruit borne of the Spirit of God.

Peace With God

There are two applications of peace in the Bible: the first is *Peace with God*, and the second is *The Peace of God*. The first is relational between man and God, and the second is intra-relational as God brings His own peace into man's heart.

To understand Peace with God we must reflect on the condition of Adam's race. Sin had divorced man from God; and man, who did not want to retain God in his knowledge, and who changed the glory of God into base images—made God his enemy.

This enmity was demonstrated by God as He first gave the Law to Israel. Within the offerings was a peace-offering which God commanded to be offered. This offering was a deliberate sacrifice to promote peaceful relations with the Deity. It also focused the light of prophecy upon the true peace-offering, Jesus Christ. In Romans 5:10 Paul declared: *"For if when we were enemies we were reconciled to God by the Death of His son, much more, we shall be saved by his life."*

He had begun this same chapter, *"Therefore being justified by faith we have peace with God through our Lord Jesus Christ."*

Hence, we have been reconciled to God, by Christ's death and, having accepted Jesus Christ as our personal Savior—we have **peace with God**.

It is also interesting to note that the first time *Shalom*, the Hebrew word for *peace*, appears in the Bible is God's promise to Abram as He sealed His Covenant, *"Thou shalt go to thy fathers in peace; thou shalt be buried in a good old age."* The faith, of the father of faith, was resting in the salvation God would provide through the death of His Son—Abram was reconciled to God through faith—he had peace, *shalom*, with God.

The Peace of God

The Old Testament prophets looked forward to The Peace of God both nationally and personally. Through Ezekiel (37:26-27) God promised to Israel an eternal reign of peace: *"Moreover I will make a covenant of peace with them; it shall be an everlasting covenant with them; and I will place them, and multiply them, and will set my sanctuary in the midst of them for evermore . . . I will be their God and they shall be my people."*

Isaiah prophesied (9:6-7) of a *"child"* that would be born Who would be named *The Prince of Peace*. He will be king and introduce a kingdom of peace that has no end. Then in the fullness of time (Galatians 4:4) this child was born—born of a virgin to redeem those under the judgment of law that we might receive the adoption of sons. The term *adoption of sons* looks beyond our spiritual birth to the time we receive our new bodies and enter into our inheritance—where the *shalom* of God rules for ever and ever.

However, it is also true that The Peace of God can rule our lives as children of God today. Remember, Jesus promised His disciples (John 14:27), *"My peace I give unto you . . . ."* Jesus, the Prince of Peace, Who is our peace, now wants peace to reign and to continually increase with each passing day. Since peace is fruit of Christ's Spirit reigning in our lives, He is changing us day-by-day into Christ-likeness.

The word translated *peace* in our New Testament has several shades of meaning. First, it describes the harmonious relationship between God and man accomplished through the Gospel. Second, it conveys a sense of rest and contentment. Third, it depicts a harmonious relationship between people and nations. Fourth, it expresses freedom from molestation. Fifth, it portrays an orderly state of being.

As peace grows within our life it will include all of these connotations of meaning. My relationship with God will become more intimate and we will spend more time together. I will refuse fear and frustration and develop excellent order in my daily life. My life will develop a greater quietness and contentment as I rest my cares on Jesus. My relationship with family, friends, acquaintances, and even strangers will become more harmonious. This is a picture of peace—fruit of the Spirit—likeness of Jesus growing and developing in my life.

Maintaining Peace

From our lessons of Spiritual Formation we are beginning to comprehend that God desires the *inward,* or spirit-being, to be growing in life, vitality, and character day-by-day and thereby controlling the *outward* man. This growth takes place (2 Corinthians 4:18) as we fix our attention *not on things that are seen, but which are not seen.* Spiritual growth needs to be planned, cultivated, and practiced. We must desire to mature spiritually, develop a course of discipline and cultivation, refuse to act on the whims or desires of the

> Spiritual growth needs to be planned, cultivated, and practiced.

old flesh which lives by what is seen, and daily put into practice what God wills and desires for our life.

Maintaining the Peace of God within our lives needs our fixed attention. The writer of Hebrews in his benedictory prayer for these scattered Jewish Christians (13:20-21) prayed that the God of peace who raised Jesus from the dead would make them perfect in every good work to do His will, working what is well-pleasing in His sight through Jesus Christ. This expresses the certainty of God's desire for them, and that He is working in them to perfect the *inward man* which will then control the *outward man.*

A similar thought is expressed by Paul writing to the Thessalonians (5:16-24) after he had exhorted them to rejoice, to pray, to give thanks for all things, and to abstain from all appearance of evil, he prayed: *"And the very God of peace sanctify you wholly, and I pray God your whole spirit, soul and body will be preserved blameless unto the coming of our Lord Jesus Christ."*

Here is a demonstration that God is working to make us holy as He is holy. As God's Spirit does His work of sanctification within our person, God desires that not only will our *inward* person grow and develop, but He is working in us that our entire spirit, soul, and body be blameless. Peter (2 Peter 3:14), after he admonished his readers to look for a new heaven and a new earth wherein righteousness dwells, admonished them to *"be diligent that ye may be found of him in peace, without spot, and blameless."* This diligence involves discipline, firm choices, and prayer.

Paul reminded the saints in Colossae (Colossians 3:10-15) that they had put off the old man with his deeds, and had put on a new man which was being renewed in the knowledge of God. He then called upon them to live lives displaying the fruit of the Spirit of God including charity, kindness, meekness, longsuffering, and then he commanded: *"Let the peace of God rule in your hearts . . . ."* The Peace of God must govern a life in which the Prince of Peace rules to do only those things that please God.

The word for "rule" in Colossians 3:15 was also used

> The Peace of God must govern (referee) a life in which the Prince of Peace rules to do only those things that please God.

for the referees in the sports arena. Whenever fears, or frustrations, or problem people disturb our peace, we must call on The Peace of God to blow the whistle and call foul—to turn us back to the will of God.

The Old Testament prophet Isaiah (26:3) also prescribed the maintenance of peace in our lives. *"Thou shall keep him in perfect peace whose mind is stayed on thee; because he trusteth in thee."*

An aura of peace surrounds our life and we rest in peace and tranquility while our mind is stayed on God. As we learned in Lesson Nine our lives are transformed by the renewing of our mind, and a life of calm, quietude, and peace are maintained by a mind saturated with His word, a prayer life before His throne, and a spirit totally immersed in His Spirit.

Dear Christian friend, wouldn't it be wonderful to have an epitaph engraved on your grave stone: This was a man (or woman) of Peace—blessed are the peacemakers, they are the children of God!

Living in an aura of peace, emanating both peace with God and the peace of God is a sure sign that we are maturing into the character and likeness of Jesus Christ.

Living in an aura of peace, emanating both peace with God and the peace of God is a sure sign that we are maturing into the character and likeness of Jesus Christ.

Lesson Twelve
Cloning the
Character of Christ

C haracter is defined as the aggregate features and traits that form the individual nature of a person or thing. The character of Jesus Christ can only be understood as we observe every action of His life and delineate each character trait displayed. By viewing these we see how the features of human nature blended with the character traits of deity are portraying God ensconced in human form and a perfect man living out the character of God.

As we seek to grow in Christ-likeness we understand more and more that the Spirit of God is renewing our mind, developing our internal character components, and guiding us to act in a godlike fashion. We have already recognized that He has borne His fruit of love, joy, and peace within our inner being. These are the basic attributes of character that govern all of our actions.

Paul has listed (Galatians 5:22-23) the fruit of the spirit as *"Love, joy, peace, longsuffering, gentleness, goodness, faith, meekness, temperance . . . ."* We have already described the first three as basic attributes of this new character God is forming in our *inward person*. We will now discuss how the remaining six are overt actions which project the character through what we call character traits of our personal nature.

A Projection of Love on the Screen of Life

There are two words describing demonstrable actions or behavior which are very closely associated. The first is the word longsuffering, and the other is patience. Longsuffering is that quality of self-restraint in the face of provocation which does not hastily retaliate or promptly punish. It is the opposite of anger, and is associated with mercy. Patience is the quality that does not surrender to circumstances or succumb under trial, it is the opposite of despondency and is associated with hope.[1]

Longsuffering is used of both God and man, but *patience* is used only of man. The Psalmist (86:15) described God: *"But thou, O Lord, art a God full of compassion, and gracious, longsuffering, and plenteous in mercy and truth."*

As Moses waited on the mountain (Exodus 34:6) to receive the ten commandments, God descended in a cloud and introduced Himself, *"The LORD, the LORD God, merciful and gracious, longsuffering, and abundant in goodness and truth."* Peter described (2 Peter 3:9) the longsuffering nature of God as he spoke of scoffers in the last days scorning the promise of Christ's coming:

> *The Lord is not slack concerning his promise, as some men count slackness; but is longsuffering to us-ward, not willing that any should perish, but that all should come to repentance.*

This is the same attitude expressed by God in the

---

[1] (Notes on Thessalonians, by Hogg and Vine, pp. 183, 184) Vine's Expository Dictionary of Biblical Words, 1985, Thomas Nelson Publishers.

days of Noah (1 Peter 3:20) when the *longsuffering* of God waited while the ark was being constructed. The longsuffering of God is demonstrated throughout the Bible as delaying judgment for sin in a merciful action providing man an extended time to repent.

It is this same merciful self-restraint, God wants to build into our new nature as people provoke us by sins against us or gross sins against God. Longsuffering is a product of love as Paul described it in the great love chapter of our Bible (1 Corinthians 13:4) *"Charity suffereth long and is kind."* It comes from the same kind of love attributed to God, as He extended salvation through the death of His own Son. He now wants love's response in your actions toward people to exhibit *longsuffering.* Peter admonished his readers (2 Peter 3:11-15) in the face of persecution and ill treatment by people, to demonstrate holy conversation and godliness—to be found in Christ without spot and blameless understanding that the long-suffering of our Lord is salvation.

Ponder for a moment the status of the character trait of *long-suffering* in your life. If *longsuffering* is the opposite of anger toward problem people, can you say of your actions that you characteristically restrain your anger and retaliation to extend mercy and desire the salvation or repentance of those troublesome people? If your *longsuffering* is falling short, will you allow, and even ask, the Holy Spirit to bear this fruit in your life and actions?

A Projection of Peace on the Screen of Life

Patience is not an oft noted characteristic of the population of Adam's children. We often resist our circumstances and fret and fume against every change to our lifestyle or environment. A life-sized illustration of patience might be the most significant demonstration of the child of God within us who is diligently laboring to become more like Jesus day-by-day.

We have already defined *patience* as the quality that does not surrender to circumstances or succumb under trial, it is the opposite of despondency and is associated with hope. There are two great posits of faith that are foundation stones of *patience*. The first is that God is in control of all my circumstances, and second, that He will allow only what is best for me. If we truly embrace these Biblical truths, then we will allow the *peace of God to rule in our lives.*

James, writing to Jewish Christians scattered by persecution, (James 1:1-4) instructed them on the value and virtue of patience. He told them to value their trials since it is a classroom for learning. The trials exercised their faith and provided circum-stances that drove them back to

> James admonishes us to value our trials since it is a classroom for our learning.

dependency upon God. Out of these trials of their faith—seeing God is faithful—patience is strengthened. He then admonished: *"Let patience have her perfect work that you may be perfect and entire, wanting nothing."* The virtue of graduating from the classroom of patience is to become a fully mature son or daughter of sovereign God.

Throughout the New Testament there are different circumstances in which we will need patience so we will obtain the hope that is set before us. The first circumstance is when we experience trials and our faith is tested. In Romans 12:12 we are encouraged to rejoice in hope while we are patient in tribulation. James (1:12) describes the person that is patient, or endures, temptations and trials as a blessed man who will receive a crown of life. Jesus, in both Matthew and Luke described the final days of apostasy on the earth prior to His return. In Luke 21:19 it is translated, *"In your patience possess ye your souls,"* and in Matthew 24:13 it is translated, *"But he that shall endure to the end, the same shall be saved."* In both of these the hope that faith envisions is that which provides patient endurance through the trial.

Trials associated with ministry are also addressed by Paul—in several epistles he enumerated the characteristics necessary to adequately proclaim the Gospel in the face of sufferings and trials. In each of these listings he named the need for patience.

Sometimes it is even possible to be treated harshly when we have done no error, Peter (1 Peter 2:20-21) tells us to take it patiently for this is acceptable with God. He then points to the example of Christ who *"suffered for us, leaving us an example that we should follow his steps."*

One of the greatest lessons on patience is given in Hebrews 12. The verbal picture is a sports arena with the stands full of the veterans of faith from the previous chapter. We are commanded to lay aside every weight and every sin that could distract us, and to run with *patience* the race that stretches before us. "*Looking unto Jesus the author and finisher of our faith, who for the joy that was set before him endured the cross, despising the shame, and is set down at the right hand of the throne of God*" (verse 2).

The writer of Hebrews (12:7-11) speaks of God's chastening as a Father correcting some behavior in His sons, and he tells us to endure it, or to be patient, knowing that God is chastening us that we might be partakers of His holiness. The word translated here as *endure* is the same word we have been studying as *be patient*, and once again the hope set before us is that of becoming holy as our Father is holy.

Gentleness, Goodness, Faithfulness

Living the Christian life is not a passive experience, it is a struggle of flesh and spirit. Bearing the fruit of the Spirit within our Christian life is not passive either, even though the Spirit of God dwells in us and we have the mind of Christ. It is a moment by moment conflict with the ego-desire of our soul and with the drives and appetites of our body; and although we have been "*strengthened by might by His Spirit in the inner man*" (Ephesians 3:16), there must be the active participation of our mind and spirit with the Holy Spirit to gain ascendancy over the flesh.

If the flesh is not brought under the control of the mind, as the body grows older it will also cast a pall of weakness, frailty and decadence over the mind and spirit to rob us of any joy, fulfillment, and patience—thus making aging miserable.

Peter addresses this active participation with the Spirit of God (2 Peter 1:3-4) first by reminding us that we are given promises of great value, that we might be partakers of divine nature. In other words God has given us everything necessary that we might be participants in divine nature, or the very character of God, and escape the corruption in this world caused by evil desires. He then instructs us (verses 5-7) to give all diligence, or work real hard:

Add to your faith virtue, and to virtue knowledge. And to knowledge temperance; and to temperance patience; and to patience godliness, and to godliness brotherly kindness; and to brotherly kindness charity.

Adding Gentleness

Peter said to add to our faith the character traits of God which we know as the fruit of the Spirit. We have addressed the fruit of the Spirit as outlined in Galatians 5:22, 23 and we come to *gentleness*. The word translated *gentleness* in this passage is also translated *kindness* in other passages of the New Testament. The Greek word means goodness, kindness, benignity and stands in contrast to a crabby, harsh disposition.

> Gentleness is a character trait grounded within the personality that conveys sweetness of temper, calmness of spirit, and a genuine politeness in all situations.

This is a character trait grounded within the personality that conveys sweetness of temper, calmness of spirit, and a genuine politeness in all situations. This kindly disposition reaches out to persons around us and seeks to aid, comfort, and assist them. It is another outward response of caring love.

One very interesting word-picture is given in the Old Testament (Proverbs 31:26) description of the ideal wife. It describes her as one who openeth her mouth with wisdom; and in her tongue is the law of kindness. This concept elevates kindness from just a word or action to a "law" or that which controls and governs her words, and demonstrates that kindness is not only what a person does but what a person is.

Gentleness and Kindness is a character trait of God that He desires to fully mature within our *inner man* and change the pattern of life of our *outer man*. The shortest Psalm (117) addresses the Gentile world. The preceding Psalm was a hymn of thanksgiving in the courts of the Lord's house for Israel and ends in a swelling praise utterance of hallelujah. Now all nations, and all peoples are invited to praise Him for His *merciful kindness* and for His *enduring truth*. It is this *merciful kindness* that sent Jesus Christ to die for all people and still longs for people of all nations to enter into His great salvation.

One of the greatest evidences that God truly lives in the life of an aging Christian is the demonstration of sweet kindness in all that we say and do.

I will never forget my mother ingraining the concept of kindness into my early childhood. As a preschool child I had an argument—probably a real fight with my sister when she came home from school. After stopping the fight my mother talked to us about the error of our behavior. I don't remember what she did about my sister, but she sat down in a rocking-chair, I laid down on the floor with my feet in her lap and there I memorized Ephesians 4:32: *"And be ye kind one to another, tenderhearted, forgiving one another, even as God for Christ's sake hath forgiven you."*

Throughout my life this imagery has come back to me scores of times when I have been tempted to treat another with harshness or rudeness—*be ye kind, tenderhearted . . . even as God . . . .*

Adding Goodness

The greatest responsibility of the Christian is to be like God. Goodness is probably the most sweeping and all inclusive characteristics of God. The concept of God as *good* and the prominence given to *good* and *goodness* are distinctive themes of the Bible. "God's goodness consists of righteousness, holiness, justice, kindness, grace, mercy, and love[1];" and God calls His children to this same distinctive goodness as a characteristic of life. Jesus commanded His followers (Matthew 5:48): *"Be ye therefore perfect, even as your Father which is in heaven is perfect." Perfect* means complete, and being complete in *goodness* is certainly a picture replicating the *image and likeness of God* in our life and lifestyle.

Paul, writing to the Ephesian Christians (5:1-9), admonished them to be followers of God as dear children. He told them to walk in love and to avoid all the sins of the flesh since they who were in past times children of disobedience, were now children of light. He then

---

[1]Nelson's Illustrated Bible Dictionary, Copyright © 1986, Thomas Nelson Publishers

summarized the fruit of the Spirit as consisting of *"all goodness and righteousness and truth."*

This entire discourse of Peter (2 Peter 1:5-7) telling us to add virtue, knowledge, temperance, patience, godliness, kindness and love to our faith reminds me of a recipe. Since we have just added *goodness* it is time to stir well over a low heat of prayer. Let's think about being a good person and practicing good deeds to all we meet. Let's aspire to constantly be good—good like God!

Adding Faith

In the paragraph above we quoted Peter telling us to add several character traits to our *faith.* Now we are going to discuss adding *faith.* Peter used *faith* as the component of our belief structure, or our foundational structure of trust, that attaches itself to God (Hebrews 11:6) believing that He is and that He is a rewarder of them who diligently seek Him. On the other hand, faith as used in Galatians 5:22 identifies it as fruit of the Spirit. It is now describing the character trait of *faithfulness.* This is describing likeness to the God side of faith—*faithfulness.*

The Faithfulness of God. As we study these character traits of God it almost seems that each one grows in stature over the last one. God's faithfulness is one of the most striking evidences of His love to Israel and to all mankind. Man dishonored His glory, refused to be thankful to Him and yet He loved them. Israel disobeyed Him, turned their backs upon Him, fashioned other gods to worship—yet He claimed them as His own. You and I have failed Him time after time, and yet, even in our declining years, when we have used up much of our time and strength, He still wants to conform us to the *Image (likeness) of Christ.*

God's faithfulness provides the pattern, model, and strength by which the life of the faithful person is to be directed. As Moses addressed the new generation that had been born in the wilderness wanderings giving them the words and laws of God as they would soon enter the Promised Land, he emphasized the faithfulness of God. Moses had certainly learned God's faithfulness by forty years of dire experiences leading an unfaithful people who nearly daily were unfaithful to God. He described God's love in choosing them (Deuteronomy 7:9) and he told them:

> *Know therefore that the LORD thy God, he is God, the faithful God, which keepeth covenant and mercy with them that love him and keep his commandments to a thousand generations.*

Later in his message (32:4), Moses broke into a song, which would become the theme of many songs eulogizing the greatness of God, *"He is the Rock, his work is perfect: for all of his ways are judgment: a God of truth and without iniquity, just and right is he."* The phrase "God of truth" uses the Hebrew word for *faithfulness.* He was declaring He is a faithful God Who does no wrong.

The Psalmist (33:4) takes up this same theme and declares that the word of the Lord is upright and all His work is done in faithfulness. Again in Psalm 119:89-90, the anthem was raised:

> *Forever, O LORD thy word is settled in heaven. Thy faithfulness is unto all generations: thou hast established the earth, and it abideth.*

The singer plucked his instrument of ten strings (Psalms 92) and extolled:

It is a good thing to give thanks unto the LORD, and to sing praises unto thy name, O most High; to show forth thy lovingkindness in the morning and thy faithfulness every night.

Even the weeping prophet in the direful dirge of Lamentations (3:22-23) declared:

It is of the LORD's mercies that we are not consumed, because his compassions fail not. They are new every morning: great is thy faithfulness.

This is the faithful God who is seeking for a man or woman to reflect His faithfulness in life and character.

God's Faithfulness Reflected in Christ

In the prophetic whisper from the Old Testament (Psalm 40:8-10) the coming Christ announced: *"I delight to do thy will, O my God, thy law is within my heart . . . I have preached righteousness . . . I have declared thy faithfulness and thy salvation."*

As He prepared to be the Lamb of God to take away the sin of the world, He prayed to His Father: *"I have glorified thee on the earth: I have finished the work which thou gavest me to do"* (John 17:4). In other words, I have been faithful to your will. The record followed His faithful life (Hebrews 2:1-2): *". . . consider the Apostle and High Priest of our profession, Christ Jesus; who was faithful to him that appointed him, as also Moses was faithful in all his house."*

In the final chapters of earth's ages (Revelation 19) the heavens will burst open and a kingly figure upon a white horse will charge toward earth's arrayed armies. His eyes are like fire, crowns are on His head and He is called **Faithful** and **True**. This is the Lord of lords and King of kings—our faithful Lord.

God's Training School of Faithfulness

God's first description of man's role (Genesis 1:26) was that he would have dominion over all the earth. Man was to take care of God's creation—to be a steward of God's possessions. After sin took possession of man he inverted this stewardship responsibility to self-interest and greed. As a new creation we are children of God and once again have the privilege and responsibility of caring for God's possessions. We brought nothing into this world and we will carry nothing out. Between the first breath and the last—we work, earn, and seek to possess, but all we have or accumulate belongs to God. These assets we manage for God fall into three categories: (1) physical assets, (2) human resources, and (3) spiritual assets. The physical assets include lands, houses, supplies, money and treasures. Human resources include children, dependencies, people we manage, and the needy who touch our lives. Spiritual assets for which we are responsible include the Word of God, time and opportunities, and the will of God. Over all of these assets which God has given each of us to manage, God expects us to exercise faithful stewardship.

The teachings of Jesus contain many references to stewards and servants. Once when He was teaching (Luke 12) His disciples He asked, *"Who is that faithful and wise steward, whom the lord shall make ruler over his household?"* He then answered this question by saying that the servant will be blessed whom the lord will find faithful to his responsibilities when he comes. But if the servant believes the lord is delaying his coming and begins to be lax with his responsibilities, the lord will judge and punish when he comes.

On another occasion (Luke 16) Jesus told a story of an unjust servant and then concluded His teaching with this statement:

He that is faithful in that which is least is faithful also in much; and he that is unjust in the least is unjust also in much. If therefore ye have not been faithful in the unrighteous mammon, who will commit to you true riches.

There are a couple very practical lessons for us of how God tests and teaches faithfulness. He gives us little responsibilities and when we prove faithful, He will give us larger responsibilities. He also gives responsibilities over physical assets to see if we can be trusted with spiritual assets. God's school of training always provides greater responsibilities to those who prove faithful in smaller responsibilities. God wants us to grow in faithfulness, and His pattern of faithfulness is the Lord Jesus Christ.

> **God's school of training always provides greater responsibilities to those who prove faithful in smaller responsibilities.**

We Are Stewards—We Are Servants

As long as God leaves us on earth with functioning faculties, we are stewards of some asset for God. The things we think of as our possessions are to be used to gain the greatest eternal impact. The people God places in our pathway can be influenced for good and for God by our words, our assistance, and the demeanor of our life.

Paul encouraged us (1 Corinthians 4:1-2) to live faithful lives so others will vouch for us: *"Let a man so account of us, as of the ministers of Christ, and stewards of the mysteries of God. Moreover it is required in stewards, that a man be found faithful."*

Perhaps faithfulness has already become a practiced trust of God's possessions and God's mysteries—the unseen things of spiritual reality. Whether we are still learning faithfulness, or whether we are continuing our patterns of faithfulness, we need to look at each moment of each of our days to see if it contains God's opportunity to be a faithful steward either in word or deed.

A Perfect Man—Measured by the Stature of Christ

The Christian who is maturing in his Spirit-directed life is described by the Apostle Paul (Colossians 3:9-10) as having put off the old man with his deeds, *"And have put on the new man, which is renewed in knowledge after the image of him that created him."* The words *put on* mean to sink down into a new garment. In the next couple verses of this same passage Paul instructs us as the elect of God, to *put on,* and he identifies the fruit of the spirit. We have studied seven of the nine fruit of the Spirit named in Galatians 5:22-23. Each of these have identified character traits of Jesus and His Father, and as this fruit is borne in our lives we are being conformed to the character of Christ. We have defined character as the aggregate of features and traits that form the individual nature of a person. By incorporating each of these character traits into our person, we are not only replicating the character of Christ we are

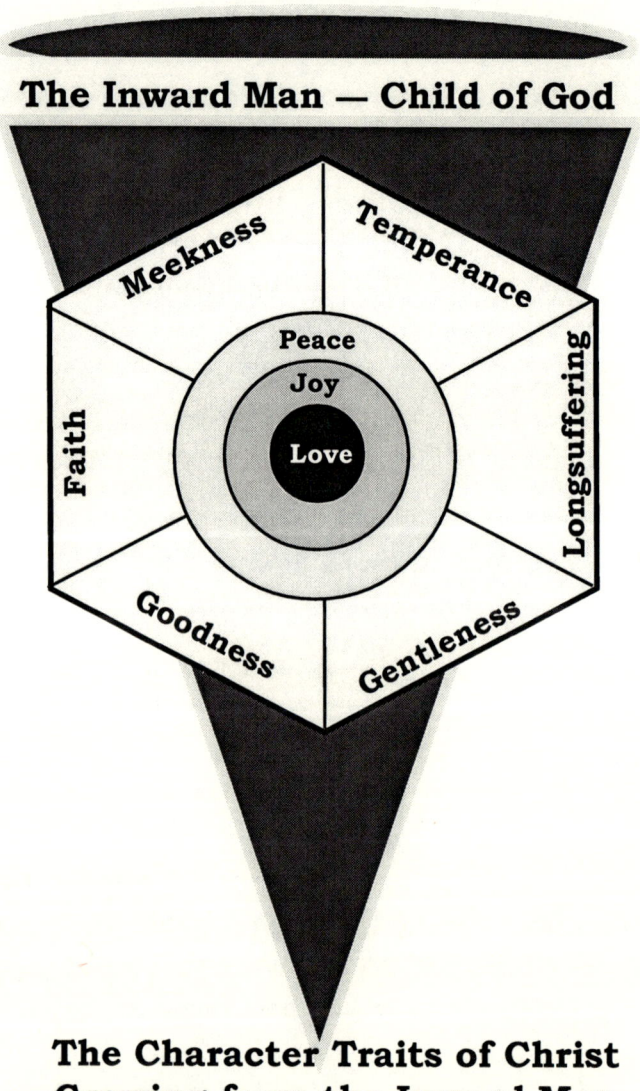

**The Character Traits of Christ
Growing from the Inward-Man**

demonstrating God's holiness through the old, worn-out and threadbare body.

The preceding chart is an attempt to symbolize the character traits of a Christian who has faithfully *put-on* the new man. Within the inward man the fruit of the Spirit has been growing outward. Notice that love, joy, and peace are the inner attributes of the spiritual person which drive and motivate all external action. The following four character traits, longsuffering, gentleness, goodness and faith are those that evidence a particular type of action or relationship toward God, people, and our environmental circumstances.

The two remaining character traits which we have not discussed are *meekness* and *temperance*. These turn the focus upon our behavior in relation to self, which of course, influences our behavior toward others.

Meekness means to see ourselves as God sees us, understanding both our limitations and possibilities. Temperance is the ability to maintain self control.

Developing a Correct Self-image

Meekness is one of the most difficult words to comprehend. In Old Testament writings it was often associated with the oppressed and afflicted as a product of suffering. The meek were special objects of Divine regard and to them special blessings were offered. The Psalmist sang often of the meek:

> *The meek shall eat and be satisfied: they shall praise the Lord . . .(22:26); The meek will he guide in judgment: and the meek will he teach his way (25:9). But the meek shall inherit the earth; and shall delight themselves in the abundance of peace (37:11). The*

LORD lifteth up the meek: he casteth the wicked down to the ground (147:6). The Lord taketh pleasure in his people: He will beautify the meek with salvation (149:4).

Isaiah, writing (61:1) of the coming Christ, declared: *"The Spirit of the Lord God is upon me; because the Lord hath anointed me to preach good tidings unto the meek . . . ."* Jesus, speaking of Himself (Matthew 11:29), said, *"I am meek and lowly in heart . . ."* Do you notice from these writings the special place the meek have in the heart of God?

To the pagan writers *meekness* often implied condescension, but to the Christian writers it implies submission. Meekness springs from a proper self-image, thoroughly recognizing that God is in control. It demonstrates a proper humility and is the opposite of self-assertiveness, and self-interest; and displays an equanimity that is neither elated nor cast down. Some would think that a man is meek because he knows he cannot help himself, but the Lord was meek because He knew He had the infinite resources of God at His command.

> **Some would think that a man is meek because he knows he cannot help himself, but the Lord was meek because He knew He had the infinite resources of God at His command.**

The New Testament writings are replete with special calls to the people of God to demonstrate meekness of heart. Paul implored his readers (Ephesians 4:1-2) to walk worthy of their calling in all lowliness and meekness. When we see an acquaintance overtaken in a fault, we are instructed (Galatians 6:1-2) to restore such a one in the spirit of meekness, lest we also be tempted. Those, teaching the Word of God, are told (2 Timothy 2:24) not to be quarrelsome; but to instruct, even those who oppose them, in meekness. James, addressing those endowed with special knowledge, tells them, (James 3:13) to show out of a good conversation, his works with meekness of wisdom.

Just as we saw from the Old Testament that God had a special fondness for meek people, we see in the New Testament God's desire that His people demonstrate the character trait of meekness. Since God wants each of His children to be conformed to the character of Jesus, He has a special interest that we each bear the fruit of meekness.

Developing Self-Control

The word translated *temperance* is a very powerful word in the Greek language. Plato used it to express mastery both of self and other powers. The Septuagint used it to describe taking possession of strongholds. Early Christian writers used it to express the avoidance of excess on both extremes, and of control over the stronger passions. The word literally means self-control.

We have spoken in other chapters, that although we are Spirit-conceived children of God, we still live in this body where the old nature, represented by our soul and body, must be controlled—if we are to do the will of our Father. The *inward man* must control our *outward man.* Growth and development of our inward-being, while residing in the garment of the earthly, must master the flesh and take possession of all carnal strongholds.

We discussed the fall of man in Lesson Two and we witnessed (Romans 1:24,26,28) God turning man over to be controlled by the psychological ego-desire system, the biological drive-system, and the apostate mind. The two control systems with which the Christian still must struggle are (1) ego-desires and (2) the drives and appetites of the flesh. Natural man wants self to be fulfilled and drives to be satisfied. Now by the power of the Spirit of God we are both instructed and commanded to refuse our soul's clamor to have its own way, and our bodies outcry to be satisfied. Instead, we are instructed (1 Corinthians 10:31) *"whether therefore we eat or drink, or whatsoever we do, do all to the glory of God."*

This control of one's self is what Paul teaches in Romans 6, 7, and 8. Based on the fact (6:6) that we have been crucified with Christ freeing us from the power of sin, we are commanded (6:12-13) to refuse sins use of our body members. We then submit these members to God so that we may bear fruit unto holiness (6:22). The continual repetition of this refusal and submittal is called (8:4,5) walking *not after the flesh,* but walking *after,* or by means, of *the Spirit.*

This continuous day-by-day, and moment-by-moment, living not *after the flesh,* but living *after the Spirit,* bears the fruit of the Spirit and causes us to be conformed to the likeness of Jesus Christ. This is the day-by-day renewal of the *inward man.*

Peter urges us (2 Peter 1:5,6) that with all diligence we add virtue to faith, and knowledge to virtue. He then admonishes *"and to knowledge temperance."* This self-control in every experience and circumstance of our life is the fruit of the Spirit that truly opens the door to godly living and holiness.

Paul uses the illustration of the sports arena (1 Corinthians 9:24-27) where the athletes are competing for a trophy. He states that every man that striveth for the mastery is temperate, or self-controlled, in all things. The athlete does it for an earthly trophy but we are competing for an incorruptible crown. Paul then describes his own discipline stating that he is not

> . . . every man that striveth for the mastery is temperate, or self-controlled, in all things.

competing aimlessly but that he is constantly controlling his body and bringing it into subjection, so that after he has preached to others he himself would not be disqualified.

Not only does he address young athletes to be self-controlled, but he also (Titus 2:2) instructs pastor Titus to teach older men to be honorable, serious, and self-controlled demonstrating the fruit of faithfulness, love, and patience.

As we turn the final lap in our race of life and see, by faith, the finish line, let us keep our self-desires and bodily drives under control as the Spirit of God perfects His fruit (Galatians 5:22,23) of love, joy, peace, patience, kindness, goodness, faithfulness, meekness, and self-control. *"If we live in the Spirit, let us also walk in the Spirit."*

If God is working in our lives to conform us to the likeness of His Son (Romans 8:29) then it follows that

He desires each of us to be a mature replica of Jesus. Paul, writing to the Church in Ephesus (4:13-15), holds up the goal of maturing into a likeness of Christ as measured by the stature of the fullness of Christ. In the same passage he compares their past condition to children and challenges them to grow up into Christ, or perhaps Christlikeness.

Our study of the fruit of the Spirit has been to analyze the character traits God desires to produce within our lives and to encourage us to give full attention to making these the maturity goals of our life.

Paul describes us, (2 Corinthians 3:18) as we gaze on God, as being *"changed into the same image from glory to glory . . . .* As God returns our gaze and looks on us, I wonder, does He exclaim, "This was what I intended when I first said, Let us make man in our image, after our likeness!"

But we all, with open face
beholding as in a mirror
the glory of the Lord,
are changed into the same image
from glory to glory,
even as by the Spirit of the Lord.

2 Cor 3:18

Lesson Thirteen

Let Us Hear the Conclusion of the Whole Matter:

Fear God and keep His Commandments for this is the whole duty of man

(Ecclesiastes 12:13)

This is the epitome of Life, or, summation, or today we would say, "bottom line" that the wise king-philosopher, who had given himself to search out wisdom, madness and folly, concluded.

This is the single antidote Solomon found to self-centered creature idols and vanities, whether expressing self-righteousness (7:16,18), or other evils (8:12-13), or mirth-madness (2:2; 7:2-5), or insatiable avarice (8:13, 17), or yet the rebellious complaining and discontent of ungodly youth (11:9, 12:1). This antidote is both an attitude and an action—fear God, and do what He commands.

"*Fear*" is unfettered reverential awe; and "*keep His Commandments*" is the unrestrained effort to do what he wills. This reverential fear and awe is developed in the mind and soul as one learns more and more about God; and keeping the commands of God are increasingly motivated both from the knowledge of God and the understanding of His will.

The entire Old Testament was the curriculum of God for Israel to seek to know Jehovah and to understand His Will. Paul expressed this when he declared: *"Wherefore the law was our schoolmaster to bring us unto Christ, that we might be justified by faith* (Galatians 3:24)."

When we speak of the Old Testament and the New Testament, we are referring to God's two Covenants. The word *covenant* means a formal binding agreement between two or more parties for the performance of certain promises or the recovery of certain damages.

The First Covenant between God and His earthly people extended the promise that God would bless and empower His people with His presence, provide their needs, and protect them against all enemies and harm. Man was to extend their faith to totally believe in Jehovah and keep what He commanded them. As the songwriter expressed man's response was to Trust and Obey . . . .

As man attempted to keep his side of the Covenant it became evident that he could not fully trust, neither could he keep God's commands. These transgressions became known as sins and the only recompense for those sins was death of man—the soul that sinneth it shall die. Since, life was in the blood, blood was the only payment for sin.

As we studied in earlier lessons, God provided a vast educational system under this first Covenant whereby man learned about a substitutionary sacrifice and the shedding of blood of birds, bulls, and goats, not to recompense for man's sins but to cover their sin from year to year—until God himself provided a Lamb, to take away the sins of the world.

Throughout this entire period of Old Covenant, the declaration of *God's Ultimate Intent* shined like a mission statement and a promise of sovereign God—Let us make man in Our *image*, after Our *likeness*!

The utterances of the First Covenant consummated in the plan of God to provide an adequate substitutionary sacrifice to fully compensate for the sin of man, that man might become the sons of God in their Father's image. The First Covenant was the first installment of His Ultimate Intent—man in the *Image of God* not by creation but by procreation.

The Second Covenant explodes upon earth and heaven in similar fashion as the first creation. God locates a young virgin woman in faithful compliance to His first Covenant, and with her consent, overshadows her with His presence and conceives a second race of mankind mothered by man and fathered by sovereign God.

Creation spotlighted this event with a strobe-like star blazing upon the manger birth place; and the heavens and the earth reechoing with crescendos of praise and rejoicing in the hallelujah chorus of the ages.

> God locates a young virgin woman ... and with her consent, overshadows her with His presence and conceives a second race of mankind—mothered by man—fathered by sovereign God.

This child, thus birthed, came to die as the lamb of God to take away the sins of the world. Faith again was the necessary response of man, *that whosoever believed in Him would not perish, but have everlasting life.*

This same child, grown to a man, instructing one of the teachers of Israel (John 3), summarized the teachings of the First Covenant that He would be lifted up on a cross like Moses lifted up the servant in the wilderness that *whosoever believeth in Him would not perish but have everlasting life.* He then acclaimed, unless a man be *conceived* from above he cannot see the kingdom of God.

Paul addressed this reality in 1 Cor. 15:45-47:

> And so it is written, *The first man Adam was made a living soul; the last Adam was made a quickening (life giving) spirit. Howbeit that was not first which is spiritual, but that which is natural; and afterward that which is spiritual. The first man is of the earth, earthy: the second man is the Lord from heaven.*

As the *last Adam,* Jesus died for the sins of all the world of Adam's children; but as the *second man* He came forth in resurrection as a life giving spirit—Son of God. Now as any child of Adam, by faith embraced Him as Lord and Savior-—a new spirit being, an image of God, was conceived within him or her.

This spirit-image of God is now designed to grow and develop within the womb of the soul and body to guide the soul to perfection, and control the body of flesh that the life may be lived in the *likeness* of Jesus Christ.

As the concept of man in the image and likeness of God, first formed in the mind of the sovereign Creator this goal for the life of man, burned in his mind:

Till we all come in the unity of the faith, and of the knowledge of the Son of God, unto a perfect man, unto the measure of the stature of the fulness of Christ (Eph. 4:13)

Yet there is one more step. A child of God, procreated by the sperm of God in the womb-like soul and body of a child of Adam, and whose soul is

---

A child of God, procreated by the sperm of God in the womb-like soul and body of a child of Adam, and whose soul is transformed into the likeness of Christ through the growth and development of spiritual formation—will be birthed into eternity in a spiritual body by the power of resurrection.

---

transformed into the likeness of Christ through the growth and development of spiritual formation—will be birthed into eternity in a spiritual body by the power of resurrection.

Paul, by the Spirit's revelation, described this scene: *"Behold, I show you a mystery; We shall not all sleep, but we shall all be changed, In a moment, in the twinkling of an eye, at the last trump: for the trumpet shall sound, and the dead shall be raised incorruptible, and we shall be changed. For this corruptible must put on incorruption, and this mortal must put on immortality (1 Cor. 15:51-53)."*

In that eternal moment, basking in the smile of sovereign God, our Father—the Ultimate Intent of God, man in the *image* and *likeness* of God, expressed from that first instant of time—will be finalized!

Conclusion for the Second Covenant

The conclusion for the earthly created people of the Old Covenant was *"fear God and keep His Commandments";* but the New Covenant is for God's heavenly procreated people. As sons and daughters of sovereign God they are to love their Father, with whom they are joined in one Spirit, and glorify Him in their body—Whether therefore ye eat, or drink, or whatsoever ye do, do all to the glory of God (1 Cor. 6:20 and 10:31).

Till we all come in the unity of the faith, and of the knowledge of the Son of God, unto a perfect man, unto the measure of the stature of the fulness of Christ: . . . speaking the truth in love, growing up into him in all things, which is the head, even Christ (Eph 4:13-15).

Conclusion for the First Covenant:
Fear God and Keep His Commandments . . .

Conclusion For the Second Covenant:
Love your heavenly Father, and whatsoever you do—do all for the glory of God.

A Final Conclusion About Spiritual Formation

The single greatest truth that a Christian must seek to completely understand is that sovereign God has conceived a new spirit being within his or her human frame. This spiritual fetus, containing the spiritual DNA of God, is in the *image* and *genus* of God. John tells us (1 John 3:9): *Whosoever is born (conceived) of God doth not commit sin; for his seed remaineth in him: and he cannot sin, because he is born (conceived) of God.*

Next, the Christian must understand that God has sent his Spirit to indwell us to illuminate and teach us, empower us, and guide us, to grow up into the *likeness* of Jesus Christ. To do this our mind must be renovated to recognize that we are dead to sin, and to refuse to allow either the psyche or body to perform the acts of sinning. Hence, this psyche must be transformed and this body controlled that we grow into the *likeness* of our Father, God. This entire transformational progress is the result of spiritual formation within us.

Ponder these two familiar verses from Romans 12:1-2: *I beseech you therefore, brethren, by the mercies of God, that ye present your bodies a living sacrifice, holy, acceptable unto God, which is your reasonable service.*

And be not conformed to this world: but be ye transformed by the renewing of your mind, that ye may prove what is that good, and acceptable, and perfect, will of God.

Note carefully, your transformation into the likeness of Jesus Christ is the good, acceptable, and perfect will of God. God's declaration of His Ultimate Intent, standing at the doorway to time, was an expression of His sovereign Will; and now your will must give assent to your intent!

My
Solemn Covenant
to Achieve

The Likeness
of
Jesus Christ

My Solemn Covenant With My Father

Whereas, I desire to live my life for the glory of God, and

Whereas, I believe that God has procreated me in His Image and of His genus. and

Whereas, this new being is in a body of clay with the soul (psyche) of Adam, but whereas Christ's death frees me from the penalty of death, and His resurrected life frees me from the power of sin, and

Whereas, God has given His spirit of Holiness to indwell, enlighten, instruct, and transform me into the likeness of Jesus Christ:

Therefore, I solemnly covenant before God my Father:

1. Not to fix my attention on what is seen but on what is unseen—not the earthly, but the eternal—not on human wisdom but on God's word—and with this careful attention, to seek to sort the worthwhile from the worthless.

2. To live not for self-desire or self-satisfaction, not for self-fulfillment or self-comfort, but to live for the growth, development, and spiritual formation of my *inward man* who has been fathered by sovereign God, and for the eternal welfare of all other lives I touch.

3. To seek with all my being to be like Jesus Christ and work together with the Spirit of holiness who

indwells me to develop the character traits of God and constantly display them through the words and deeds of the *outward man* until we all come in the unity of the faith, and of the knowledge of the Son of God, unto a perfect man, unto the measure of the stature of the fullness of Christ!

In total dependence upon the Spirit of God who indwells me, I affix my signature to this Covenant, and solemnly pledge to glorify my heavenly Father by demonstrating His Image and Likeness in all my thoughts, words, and actions before the watching world.

_____

Date: _____ ____, 20___

CPSIA information can be obtained
at www.ICGtesting.com
Printed in the USA
FSOW02n1524120917
38448FS

9 781640 458031